Reviews of *The King*

"FRESH, INSPIRING, TRUE - and most of all, pr give lots of great thoughts and theories for you to ponder and mull over, but that is generally where they stop. Paul expertly puts practical application of well thought out ideas into your head that you can take out and use immediately. Get ready to enter the Kingdom mindset, challenge yourself, and get tons of encouragement as you read Paul's writing." Walker Clan - 5 Stars

"REAL FAITH...REAL TEACHING - This book series is continually encouraging the every day Christian to take a step back at what is called the norm in Christian living and understand the heart behind it all. Have you ever wondered where the 'line' is in certain areas of life... like watching movies or music, helping your kids understand what is right and wrong? Paul Gibbs places Kingdom Principles to live by... not rules and regulations...liberty not slavery. Highly recommended for the Christian seeking to go further...two thumbs up!" Tim Ro - 4 Stars

"DEEP AND IMPACTFUL! - This book can help you to find the seeds that have been planted, watered, and that God is wanting to grow in you! Your purpose in life will become more clear! Through this book, I have gained so much insight into how to live the abundant life that God desires for all of us to have! To leave this world a better place than when I entered it." Stephanie - 5 Stars

"THIS IS A MUST READ - A fantastic book which really makes you think and explore ideas to a deeper level. Such a quick and easy read due to the layout and content. The personal stories told are really engaging, whilst helpful in explaining the desired point. Read this book if you want to be challenged, inspired, and encouraged - you won't regret it!" Holly - 4 Stars

"INSPIRING AND CHALLENGING BOOK - It is an easy read with simple style of writing but with deep questions and thoughts. Many times I had to just pause to process the thought or allow my mind to process the question and to unpack it...A great book that anybody choosing to live for God should read." Dan Ran - 5 Stars

"A MUST READ! - This book challenged me to dig deeper into the Father's heart as it distinguished between religion and faith. Ultimately I would recommend this book to anyone who desires to see day-to-day questions we ask through God's eyes rather than our own, strives to be an instrument in the furthering of the Kingdom of God, and yearns to be captivated by a renewed love for the Father. Overall, it was an amazing book and I would encourage you to take the time to read it!" Elle Marie - 5 Stars

"ABOVE THE LINE - If you are interested in learning about the heart of God, you need to read this book. I know a lot of people who have dismissed God because they believe He is a cosmic-killjoy, but this book will help them see the true heart of the God of the Bible and give them an appetite to dig into the Bible and gain more insight as to who God really is. It is easy to read and very thought provoking. Excellent book!!" Misha - 5 Stars

"USEFUL AND PRACTICAL - In the process of beginning anything new, fresh, or different, I think everyone goes through stages of the process. The problem is, no one knows what the stages are, until now. Paul does an excellent job of breaking down the stages of pioneering, using simple terms and analogies that are practical in nature and Biblical in scope. The best part about the book is that it is not just information, but it actually helps the pioneer in whatever stage he/she is in." Carl - 5 Stars

"BE FOREWARNED - Gibbs' challenging thoughts on vision and leadership make me uncomfortable. It is not always easy to see where I am within the four stages of pioneering, or even to see my personal vision for my efforts in the Kingdom in High Definition . . . but this story and challenge offer me a lens. It has given perspective to the early years of my journey, and in some places has unpacked the vague feelings and thoughts that were floating around in my head and my heart almost anonymously." Chris - 5 Stars

"READ IT!! - This book inspired me, moved me, and challenged me on things I had not even thought about before!" Judith - 4 Stars

"CATCHING THE PIONEERING SPIRIT - What's great about this book is that it's real stories about real people; it is their successes and failures. It is an inspirational book about a grassroots organization that has risen to have a Global influence but also gives the reader clear, practical advice. Although written from a Church ministry perspective, I can imagine that pioneers from different walks of life could find themselves in one of the four stages of a pioneer and also find hope and direction that will help enable them to take their dream into a reality." Pete - 5 Stars

"I HAVE BEEN SO BLESSED BY THE BOOK - After feeling very led to purchase it, I gave [my first copy] away after reading the first few incredible pages. Thoughts of myself said, I'm not a pioneer. I am a helper, a person who helps other people with their vision.... And then, I let God tell me what He thought of me. He brought to remembrance things placed in my heart long ago." Tifany - 5 Stars

*Reviews for The Kingdom Trilogy book series by Paul Clayton Gibbs. Used by permission from Amazon. Look for *Kingdom Principles: Develop Godly Character* and *Kingdom Patterns: Discover God's Direction* on amazon.com.

PAUL CLAYTON GIBBS

KINGDOM PIONEERING

•

fulfill God's calling

Harris House Publishing

KINGDOM PIONEERING: Fulfill God's Calling
(A previous version of this book was titled THE LINE AND THE DOT: The Kingdom Pioneers)
Copyright © 2010, 2014, 2017 by Paul Clayton Gibbs

Published by Harris House Publishing
www.harrishousepublishing.com
Colleyville, Texas
USA

Originally published in association with Pais Project Publications.
www.paismovement.com/resources

This title is also available in other formats.
Cover creation and design by Paul Green and Paul Clayton Gibbs/ revised by Dino Gilley.
Author's photo by Dino Gilley © 2014.

Internet addresses (websites, etc.) are offered as a resource to you. These are not intended as an endorsement by Harris House Publishing, nor do we vouch for the content of these sites.

Library of Congress Cataloging-in-Publication Data

Gibbs, Paul Clayton, 1964 -
        KINGDOM PIONEERING: Fulfill God's Calling / Paul Clayton Gibbs
            p.cm.
        Includes bibliographical references
        ISBN 978-1-946369-29-1 (pbk.)
        1. Christianity and Culture. 2. Christian Life. I. Title.
BR115.C8G53   2014
261 - dc22   2014955532

Printed in the United States of America.

For Lynn
my best friend
"number 9"

In memory of Doris, my mum, who gave me the spirit of a pioneer —
wish I had thanked you.

My thanks to

The Foxy Lynn for your belief in my 'it'

Joel for being so easy to love — I pray you will see the pioneer I see and admire in you

Levi for being so easy to love — I pray you will know why you have so much creativity

Dad for being someone I could always trust, respect, and want to emulate

Harry for being my pastor and letting me dye my hair red if I wanted to

Pais to my many friends who gave me a part of your life — it has been an honor

Churches — Sharon for Pais' birth, thefaithworks for its incubation, Pantego for its maturing

Sebrina for your blend of gifts; we would be waiting another 8 years if it weren't for you

Paul for your inspiring commitment to our vision and the fun you bring to us all

Mike & Becca for generously releasing me to write this book

Terry & Wayne for making the book a reality

Harris House Publishing for seeking God's Kingdom first and your business second

KINGDOM PIONEERING

The Spirit of a Pioneer

5,280

Have you ever wondered why you exist? It's simple really. You exist because God did not have anyone just like you . . . and He wanted someone *just like you*.

It therefore makes sense that you have a slightly different way of thinking about things, a subtly unique approach to a problem or opportunity. This uniqueness, this quirkiness, this inability to see things exactly like everyone else does, this creates an opportunity for God.

Your imperfection gifts you the pioneering DNA.

Now, you may not think of yourself as a pioneer . . . but I humbly disagree. It depends, of course, on how you define a pioneer. If your description is of a charismatic visionary who builds an organization or invents a new medicine, then sure, you may be right. But I believe Jesus would define a pioneer differently.

Listen to His words when advising the kind of people who will advance His kingdom:

> *If someone forces you to go one mile, go with him two miles.*[1]

A pioneer is someone who goes that extra mile . . . and then a little further.

And that is important because it is these 5,280 feet that turn promise into reality.

I have pioneered or repurposed several things in my life, and over a period of time, I have recognized a pattern in the process. Every pioneer goes on a similar journey, and if we study the route, we will be better equipped to navigate our way successfully.

This book teaches the four stages you will inevitably go through if you pursue the dreams that God puts in your heart:

> *Revelation*
> *Revolution*
> *Resistance*
> *Reproduction*

It also provides insight into four major tests you will face so that when you are confronted by the various challenges of pioneering, you will not be confused, think you have gotten it wrong, or doubt that God is in control. Instead, you will be prepared to pass the test each stage brings.

Each stage is split into three sections:

> *My Story*: my experience during this stage
> *Our Story*: an explanation of the stage
> *Your Story*: advice for you to apply during each stage

Pioneers inspire pioneers, and their stories trump their statements.

God used stories to call me to do what I do. It was the Hudson Taylors,[2] the Jackie Pullingers,[3] the Loren Cunninghams[4] of the world and their experiences that helped me realize I was shaped that way. Reading their lives taught me that pioneering is not about talent, but temperament.

Let me ask you a question. Who was the first man on the moon? Neil Armstrong, right? And what did he say?

"That's one small step for man; one giant leap for mankind."

But who was the second man on the moon? Buzz Aldrin, right? And what did he say?

Who cares!

Think about it. The people we are most interested in are not the ones with letters after their names, but the ones who created or did something new or different.

"I have a dream." – Martin Luther King, Jr.[5]

"Never in the field of human conflict was so much owed by so many to so few." – Winston Churchill[6]

"I am the way, the truth, and the life." – Jesus Christ[7]

People are first captured by their story, and only then are they influenced by their statements.

Way

Personally, the story that most inspires me to pioneer is the one of Jesus.

> Do you see what this means—all these pioneers who blazed the way, all these veterans cheering us on? It means we'd better get on with it. Strip down, start running—and never quit! No extra spiritual fat, no parasitic sins. Keep your eyes on Jesus, who both began and finished this race we're in. Study how he did it. Because he never lost sight of where he was headed—that exhilarating finish in and with God—he could put up with anything along the way . . .[8]

But Jesus was God. Surely it was easy for Him! How can you and I be pioneers?

What is interesting is that Jesus was not the first to pioneer the Kingdom of God.

> *And from the time John the Baptist began preaching until now, the Kingdom of Heaven has been forcefully advancing . . .*[9]

The Kingdom broke through with John, not Jesus.[10]

John prepared a way for Jesus. So can you.

> *A pioneer is a person or group that originates or helps open up a new line of thought or activity or a new method or technical development.*[11]

To pioneer is not to do everything yourself and on your own. It is to 'help open up.'

Imagine an old war movie where a small unit of soldiers must take the enemy's gun position. A wall of barbed wire lies between them and their objective. Many will lose their lives and the battle will be lost if the troops cannot advance. So one of the soldiers, probably the bravest, runs out and throws himself upon the barbed wire. Lying fully stretched out on top of it, his body creates a path. The other soldiers then run single file across his back in order to gain the victory.

A pioneer does not simply *find* a way; a pioneer *becomes* the way.

A pioneer creates a path for others where none previously existed.

Line

The Kingdom of God is 5,280 feet long.

It is not a geographical place. You cannot find it on a map or a Sat Nav. It does not have a GPS or a map reference. It does not have a physical start and finish. But it is best seen when it is 63,360 inches long. Or, if you're metric, 1,609.34 meters long. Or, if you lived in the days of the disciples, 1,000 paces.

The Kingdom of God appears in the extra mile.

The most significant thing you will ever do for the Kingdom of God is the one thing that no one tells you to do. It is when you go off the page of what has been written for you by others. It is when you go beyond the path set out for you.

Think about it.

What influenced an empire was not a political vote or a violent rebellion. What shocked the world was when hardened Roman soldiers, who in many different nations had forced begrudging subordinates to carry their backpacks, were suddenly stunned by a new reaction . . . followers of the Way who turned around and asked:

"Would you like me to carry it a little further for you?"

While many *run after* what they are *not* entitled to, Jesus needs those who will *run away* from what they *are* entitled to!

But why?

Well, many of us live on a line. This line represents the laws of God. These laws have a purpose. They help us know where we are failing . . . but they do not have the power to help us succeed.

As line-dwellers, we look at one end of the line and ask, *How far can we go without getting into trouble?* At the other end, we ask, *How far must we go in order to be rewarded?*

Yet these two questions limit who we can be for God and what we can do for Him.

Our fixation upon this line and its religious rules, regulations, and traditions can create barriers in our minds. It is not that we are afraid to do something *new*; it is that we are too busy trying to do what is *right*. Jesus clearly believes, however, that a different kind of question should guide us.

What if, instead of line-dwelling, we asked:

What will most advance the Kingdom of God?

The Church, when it is advancing, is the one with the new ideas: hospitals, schools, orphanages. Its purpose is not to keep and control those ideas for themselves, but to open the way for others to reproduce them.

When we pioneer, people copy us, but when we stall, we simply duplicate the world's ideas. We settle with 'sanctifying' the things which others were creative enough or passionate enough to try first, and we end up controlling new thinking rather than creating it.

When it comes to advancing the Kingdom of God, the *'Christian version of'* never works.

So, may we no longer dream dreams that are simply a cut-and-paste version of what is safe and familiar. Instead, may we see vision not as a search for an answer, but as the quest for the next question.

Jesus was, and is, looking to recruit men and women, boys and girls, who will leave their old questions far behind. People who choose to forget their rights and rewards, and instead share in the responsibility He gave us to change our world. People who are so far beyond the line where others dwell that the line is now a dot to them.

REVELATION

STAGE ONE

REVELATION | My Story

Tent

When my mother had to tie me to the bed with my bandages, I knew things were bad.

I was born with eczema, and by the time I was thirteen, the skin disease had become septic. My itchy skin would peel, revealing open, oozing sores whenever I removed my compress. It was both painful and distressing. Yet this condition launched me on a journey I would never have expected, causing me to step foot into some surprising places to share a passion I never dreamt I could have.

It started the day I first remember hearing about Jesus.

I sat squirming in my chair with yellow pus on my arms and legs as I listened to my friends tell me about 'the Tent.' The stories went something like this: people would go in, sing some strange songs, listen to someone talk, and then this man would pray for them. There was a bit of a buzz at the school because it was rumored that some of the boys who went had been healed. Sitting there in my seat, I listened as my friends simply said:

"Why don't you go? You're practically a cripple!"

I did not really believe in God, but I didn't *not* believe in God either. I had great parents, but like most young men in England at that time, I had not been brought up with a faith.

On the last day of what I later came to know as a crusade, I went with my brother. The guy speaking was called an 'evangelist.' I wondered if that was his actual name. I listened to him speak, not understanding much at all, yet something within me rose to the challenge of what he was saying.

And then he tricked me.

He said a prayer and asked anybody who wanted to respond to say the prayer with him. And so I did it. Then he said, "If you've said the prayer, put your hand up." Bemused, I raised my arm. He then said, "If you've got your hand in the air, please stand up." I found myself thinking, *This one last thing and that is it.* And so I stood.

Then the sucker punch:

> "If you're standing, please come to the back of the tent. I'd like to pray for you."

I was determined not to move, but the girl I'd been keeping my eye on throughout the service went forward, and mysteriously at that moment, I felt God call me too.

Something inside said, *If I do this, I might get healed.* But after a chat and prayer, I went back into the main part of the tent to find everyone had gone.

I left feeling strange and still itchy.

However, I was invited to attend church and offered free transport there. The first sermon I heard told me I did not need a priest; I could pray directly to God. And so I did. One week later, my skin disease had entirely gone.

I remember thinking to myself:

> *If this is true, everyone needs to know about it!*

Yet four years later, I had left the church.

Ferret

Faith is an act of will, but I was faithfully willful.

My beliefs did not change at eighteen, but my desires took over. So I separated myself from anybody or anything that could tell me what to do. I ended up in a house made up of four apartments. In my apartment was another apathetic and backslidden Christian like myself. Opposite us were three very rich college students, including one whose father was a director of a world famous London department store. Above them were a hippy and a Jehovah's Witness. Above us were three anarchists and a ferret.

That house had some very forceful people, each one trying to convert the others to their set of ideals, whether that was religion, materialism, or militant vegetarianism. Even though my beliefs had never changed, my attempts to convert others to Christianity were ineffective. I was passionate about little else but my own selfish ambitions. That was clear to them and it was clear to me.

In the three years of my life as a self-imposed spiritual recluse, I never spoke to another Christian until one particular day just after my twentieth birthday party when the police knocked on my door. Someone had overdosed on drugs and ended up in the hospital in a comatose state, so the police came to the house to investigate. The officer in charge was someone I knew, a member of the church I had gone to years earlier. Although we brushed him away, I could not brush away the presence he had brought into the house.

That was the beginning of the end. I think seeing him in some way softened what was a hardened heart. Only days later, on the top floor of a double-decker bus, from out of nowhere, I was suddenly filled with hope and joy. There was no reason for it. I certainly had not summoned it up. It was just there. Then something inside me asked the question:

Do you remember this?

I did. One month later I walked back into church, and one hour later I was following Jesus again.

Call

When I was twenty-one years old, a friend told me about a mission trip to Scotland. It was an opportunity for me to share my story and even use my love for acting. For two weeks, I was basically a spiritual performer on the streets of Edinburgh. After one week into the experience, I knew what I wanted to do with the rest of my life. I began to hear the term 'calling' spoken by various people. I had also heard the word 'missionary' and about an opportunity to train for four months to become one. The organization was called Youth With A Mission, which summed me right up.

But there was a problem. Her name was Lynn.

When someone had asked me if I believed revival would ever come, I joked that the sign would be when a girl with black spiky hair and big blue eyes walked into the church. I smiled wryly, doubting that day would ever come since I was the only 'post-punk' in our congregation. I spent my late teens shaving the side of my head, spiking my hair, and wearing black eye makeup. The chance of someone like me coming in was very, very unlikely.

But the unlikely sometimes happens.

On our first date, we crashed into a police car. It wasn't the best start to a relationship, but not long afterwards we became serious about each other. Yet I was even more serious about this wild idea of being a missionary. After we dated for a year or so, I went off to train, believing it would be the end of our relationship.[12] We remained friends, and Lynn occasionally visited me, but there seemed to be no future for us. She knew that she was not called to Africa, Asia, or somewhere even more remote and desperate, but I was convinced that I was.

It turned out I was wrong.

After my training course, the same voice that had spoken to me on the bus directed me back to Manchester. Confused as to why, I walked into my pastor's office and asked if I could do anything for him. Unsure of where I was going, I needed to start somewhere and do something. So, the following months consisted of typing letters, answering phones, visiting old ladies, and filling in gaps of day-to-day ministry for my pastor, Harry Letson. Plus, every month we went to a local ministers' meeting where I began to connect with other ministers.

It was interesting work, but it did not fulfill the desire I had to reach the world.

Beans

Then one day my world changed with a phone call.

A minister of a small youth group had some students who had been sharing their faith at school in Blackley, around five miles from where I lived in Manchester, England. Their strategy started very simply: a baked beans eating contest followed by an invitation to listen to the story of how they found Jesus. It went better than expected. Over the next few weeks, they retold their story to twenty, thirty, forty students at a time every Wednesday during lunch.

It was the largest Christian youth group I knew in Manchester. And it met in a school.

Soon, however, the students leading it would leave for college, and the lunch club would cease. The minister asked if I would meet with the school principal to see if I could carry on their work. I did, and not long after, untrained but undeterred, I began to run the 'Christian Union' which continued to grow. It was a great opportunity, but every time I walked through the corridors on my way to the upstairs room, I would look around and see several hundred students . . . the vast majority of whom had never truly heard Jesus' story.

It got me thinking. Specifically, it got me asking questions.

Why, when Jesus so clearly told us to invest in others, did our local churches spend so much time investing in ourselves? Why did we focus all our money, strategy, and time on the small number of students in our church when hundreds more were in schools where someone else was already paying for the building, staff, gas, and electricity? Why work so hard at encouraging youth to attend our building in order to mentor them, when local schools were crying out for role models?

Serving schools is not brain surgery. It's just common sense.

So I went to the Manchester Education Committee and asked for copies of their curriculum for their Personal and Social Education. As I looked through the syllabus, topics popped out that shared common values with the message of Jesus. Identity, purpose, inclusiveness, relationships—all were relevant to both the objectives of the Kingdom and of the Institute. Then I went back to the school and approached the head of PSE.

She was a Jewish lady, friendly and with a clear concern for her students.

"When you teach law and order," I said, "you invite the police to speak. When you teach health and safety, the fire service is involved. So when you teach these subjects, would you like me to provide a similar service? I could give examples, I could share stories, and I could bring a fresh voice."

During my time at school, I had learned a valuable lesson. In the religious education I'd received, I had two different teachers. They both taught about Christianity, but one turned me off of God, and one turned me on to Him. They taught the same curriculum, but one passed on a program. The second passed on his passion.

The lesson? Our beliefs don't transfer; our passions do!

The head of PSE agreed with my proposal and gave me opportunities to teach lessons. The first time I remember being introduced to a class, one teacher said, "Students, as you know, we have been going through a series teaching the myths of the world, and last week we looked at the story of Noah's Ark. Well this week, we have found someone who actually believes that happened. His name is Paul Gibbs. Let's welcome him to the class."

In a fifty minute lesson, I spent half of it trying to explain the logistics of how Noah's Ark may have happened and the other half answering questions. Questions such as, "Have you always believed this?" and "Do your parents believe this?" Questions which led to answers such as, "No, but let me tell you about my skin disease . . ." The school loved it!

Around that time, I was also involved in outreaches where I felt like I was forcing people to listen to me. In school, I was acknowledged for offering a service. It seemed to fit Jesus' model a little better.

Pais

Going the extra mile means to go beyond what has already been asked of you.

More opportunities began to present themselves. Most I created myself, but a couple of local pastors gave me some training, invitations, and help along the way.[13] About three years after the 'baked bean outreach,' I was serving around seventeen schools and teaching roughly 10,000 students per year. At some of those schools, I ran a lunch club. For some, I taught lessons on a regular basis. At others, I simply presented the occasional assembly.

It was going great, but it didn't satisfy the model I saw when I read my Bible.

There's a difference between making converts and making disciples. A restlessness was rumbling inside me. I sensed that what I was doing was only partially authentic.

Then one day, a student approached me after class. "I love your lessons," he said. "In fact, because of your lessons, my parents wanted to know more, and so they've asked these two men to come to our house one evening a week. They wear blue suits and backpacks."[14]

The challenge was obvious. If I didn't go the extra mile, someone else would. I needed to follow up with the many young people wanting a next step. And there were lots of them! Students often asked how they could find out more of what I was speaking about, and my answer was to encourage them to attend a local church. The problem was that they always asked if I would be there. In those days I could not afford a car and would walk for an hour and a half to get to some of the schools, so getting to the various churches was not a viable option.

The key, I realized, was to find others who would come into schools with me and be based at those various churches. The idea was that they would act as a relational bridge. The more I thought about my situation, the more the following five questions gnawed away at me.

> Q1: *How do I attract a large number of people to help me?*
>
> Q2: *How do I help students integrate with the local church?*
>
> Q3: *How do I get more churches directly involved?*
>
> Q4: *How can I keep the ministry fresh and varied?*
>
> Q5: *How do I help youth groups keep students?*

Eventually, these questions led me to the following answers.

> A1: *By offering FREE apprenticeships.*
>
> A2: *By training Pais Apprentices to become a relational bridge.*
>
> A3: *By Pais Apprentices serving in the church youth program.*
>
> A4: *By recruiting Pais Apprentices from various nations with a variety of talents.*
>
> A5: *By training Pais Apprentices to model mission, discipleship, and Bible study.*

After three years of experimentation, Pais was founded in September 1992. Pais is the New Testament Greek word for:

A child servant of the king.[15]

That first year, I travelled the length and breadth of Great Britain to find recruits. Serving with me on my first team was Ulle, a young German woman who played guitar; Joanne, a Bible college graduate from the south of the country; Gary, a local youth pastor; and Lisa, a high school graduate from Birmingham, England.

We were all based in different churches, but came together each morning at eight o'clock to pray and prepare. During the week, we served the schools of North Manchester, building relationships with teachers by keeping within their boundaries and offering enthusiasm, passion, and professionalism. In the evenings and on weekends, we served our different churches, coming alongside their youth pastors and other volunteers. The churches were very small and had little finances, but they found host homes with church families. Every youth group we were a part of became a home to young people looking for faith. It worked, and so I thought my vision was complete!

I was, of course . . . wrong.

I had not understood where vision really comes from.

Questions for the pioneer

1. What similarities do you see between my story and your story? Try not to look at circumstances, but principles.

2. Pick a section from *my story* and write down what you think I was feeling in that situation. If you had gone through the same situation, how would it have made you feel?

3. How do your feelings affect what comes next?

REVELATION | Our Story

Blind

Vision comes from an awkward conversation with God.

Let me explain.

One day as Jesus walked the dusty road stretching between the old and new cities of Jericho, blind Bartimaeus, the son of Timaeus, called out:

> Son of David, have mercy on me![16]

Why? Jesus was the son of Mary and Joseph.

'Son of David' meant more than being a son of a man called David. It was a label. Specifically, it was the title given to the One who would be known as the Messiah.

Bartimaeus' statement was incredible because this visually impaired man saw something that many other people had been searching for and missed.

> He was in the world, and though the world was made through Him, the world did not recognize Him.[17]

A number of groups in Jesus' day were searching for the Son of David.

The Zealots thought the Messiah would be a militaristic hero. They believed if they could stir up Israel to fight the Romans, God would send the Messiah to free them.

The Essenes had given up on Jerusalem and the Temple and had run for the hills. They lived in a holy huddle, having nothing to do with the rest of the Jews. They had their own schools, their own shops . . . essentially their own community. They believed the Messiah would recognize that only they were the sons of light.

The Pharisees were looking for a Messiah sent by a Holy God. If they could only get Israel to clean up her act and eliminate the sinners, then surely God would send the Son of David.

Yet they made the mistake so many of us make.

We miss God in our lives, not because we do not know what He looks like, but because we have decided what He looks like in advance. Then, when He arrives, we are so busy investing our time, energy, thoughts, and finances in what we expect Him to achieve, that we fail to see what He is really up to.

We invest in the wrong Jesus.

For us to see, we first have to become blind.

Bartimaeus saw with his own eyes the miracles *of* Jesus, but only after his blindness helped him recognize the miracle that *is* Jesus.

Awkward

When Bartimaeus called out to Him, Jesus asked him a question.

What do you want me to do for you?[18]

This seems like an unusual thing for Jesus to ask. Surely it is obvious. Unusual? Yes. Uncommon? No. Some Bible scholars estimate that

Jesus was asked 300 questions during His ministry and that he gave a straight answer to three. They also say that Jesus asked around 125 questions, many of which were in answer to questions He was first asked. In other words, if you asked Jesus a question, you had a one-in-three chance of being asked one in return!

Jesus was a pioneer but He was also a rabbi, and rabbis answer by asking.

Why? Perhaps the best reason is found in the true story of a tourist who was shopping in a photographer's gallery in Jerusalem. Finding it difficult to choose from all the beautiful photos, the woman decided to ask the Jewish photographer a question.

"Which one is your favorite?"

He replied, "Are you married?"

Now you might have expected her to walk out of the shop without an answer, thinking the man was very rude or quite forward. However, she had been on a tour of the city and learned that a rabbi answered questions with a question. So instead she replied, "Yes . . . Why?"

"Do you have children?" was the even more random response.

"Yes, three . . . Why?"

"Which one is your favorite?"

His third and final question contained the answer. Significantly, rather than informing her that his photographs were like children to him, he helped her *feel* what he felt about them.

The purpose of vision is not to pass on answers, but to pass on understanding.

Questions

The greatest vision comes from the greatest questions. The biggest vision comes from the biggest questions. Yet, the clearest vision comes from the most awkward questions.

If revelation comes from a conversation of awkward questions with God, then the dramatic simply gets our attention. The vision is not in the drama; the drama purely exists to help us recognize our blindness.

Think about it.

Mistakenly, we think Moses was given his vision of a burning bush. But the bush was not the vision; it simply caught his attention. His vision came from the following awkward conversation.

"I am sending you," said God.

"Why me?" asked Moses. "I'm a nobody, I can't speak well, and I know too little."[19]

Saul of Tarsus, later named Paul, who was the author of much of the New Testament, did not receive his revelation from a blinding light. No, the blinding light was just that—blinding! It took *away* his vision. His revelation also came from an awkward conversation.

"Saul, Saul, why are you persecuting Me?"

"Who are you, Lord?"[20]

Vision is developed when we see something that captures our imagination or frustration and we ask Him a question. He asks us one back, and then, hopefully, we ask another. So the principle about vision that all pioneers must learn is this:

While the questions keep coming, so does the revelation.

When the conversation stops, the vision stops.

This is why so many people are living off of old ideas. For some reason, they ceased to ask God any more questions, or they refused to answer any of His. They have effectively stalled, and their vision is no longer sharp.

Pioneer, please let me ask, what is getting your attention right now? What awkward questions do you have for God? Do not worry. He is a big God. He does not suffer from doubt or insecurity. He is not in heaven thinking, *Oh dear, I hope they don't ask me that one!*

I encourage you to ask your questions and keep asking them. But please do not walk away when you are asked something difficult in return.

God is not putting you off. He is drawing you in.

33⅓

Now for another question.

What is the better type of vision?

Well, first, pioneers need a *bigger* vision because a bigger vision changes us. A bigger vision helps us to see ourselves as bigger people because we see ourselves through a big God's eyes.

The purpose of vision is not simply to transform the world; it is to transform *you*.

I am afflicted with a mild form of dyslexia and occasionally, when I am tired, I do not pronounce my words correctly. So when I was six years old, my parents sent me to a private school for elocution (diction), movement, and dance lessons.

A short time later I was expelled . . . for biting the girls. My parents then took me to a doctor who announced, "Mr. and Mrs. Gibbs, your son is a problem child and always will be."

In high school, my nickname was 'thirty-three and a third.' I was told that my voice sounded like a single playing vinyl record, which runs at 45 RPM, being played at the album speed 33⅓. I never saw myself as a public speaker, and I certainly did not see myself as a popular speaker. Yet I speak all around the world, sometimes to tens of thousands.

Also, I never related well to young people, even when I was a young person. When teachers were late, which seemed to happen quite often, a cry would go out, *"Crucify the Christian!"* Everyone would cheer, including me, until I realized *I* was the Christian. In a class of thirty-five boys, I was the only one. After a short scuffle, one of two things usually happened. Either I would be buried under every single table and chair in the room, all piled on top of me in an artistic yet life-threatening manner, or alternatively, I would be hung from the high ceiling with ropes that were usually used to open the top windows. I never imagined I would one day lead a ministry for young people.

Vision is possibly the greatest element of change we can experience, because when we see a bigger God, we see a bigger God in us.

And so, at this first stage of revelation, we must allow vision to change us before we can change our world.

Oneighty

The greatest type of vision is not the vision a big God gives you.

It is the vision of a bigger God.

During my first trip to the States, I visited an incredible youth ministry building in Tulsa, Oklahoma.[21] My friend was excited for me to see it, and as we drove onto the campus I understood why. The building was huge. Not only huge, but the facility was contemporary and edgy in everything from technology to design. The reception area was a work of art. The snack bar was clean and sharp, rivaling any cinema in the world. In between the reception and snack bar was a basketball half-court, entirely encased in glass. On the second level were rows of iPods (still a novelty at that time) alongside rows of the latest game consoles. Behind all this was the meeting room, or sanctuary, as they called it, seating up to 1,200 teenagers every Wednesday night.

The place was, as they say in America, *awesome*.

When I showed pictures back in England, many looked at the building, rolled their eyes, and said, "Only in America!"

I was excited! What faith these American Christians must have, I thought. Just wait until they hear about schools ministry! We can reach an entire school for just a few thousand dollars, a fraction of what this building must have cost. Plus, most young people whom schools ministry reaches are not already attending church.

The American pastors I met first encouraged me.

Then they said . . . "Only in England!"

This is the problem we face. We believe that God is the God of the impossible in one area of our lives but not another. In England, we think He is the God of the impossible schools outreach but not of the impossible building. In America, we believe He is the God of the impossible building but not of the impossible schools outreach.

We are Christian in title, but pagan in thinking. The pagans believed in 'gods' of territories. A god could do miracles in one place but not another.

Yet, if God is God of the impossible in one area of our lives, He is God of the impossible in *every* area of our lives.

Theme

So what is the weaker, poorer, less powerful type of vision?

A vision of vision.

It may be a building, a numerical goal, a project, or who knows what. The problem with this is when the vision is going well, we are doing well. When the vision is going badly, we are doing badly.

Where there is no revelation, people cast off restraint.[22]

For instance, you can tell if a youth pastor has a vision of vision. On a Wednesday or a Friday night, they are incredibly passionate about their message. They are creative, sacrificial, hard-working, and plead with the young people to hear the Word of God . . . but their next-door neighbor doesn't even know they are Christian.

Or the worship pastor, who practices tirelessly and shows great dedication to motivating others to praise God . . . but is late, apathetic, and non-committed to anything another leader puts on.

A vision of vision is a cut-and-paste vision.

A vision of God, however, gives you a theme.

My vision is not the Pais Movement. My vision is not a number. My vision is not a building. My vision is not even schools work. My vision is a theme, not a target.

My theme is to make missionaries.

Having a theme means that whether I'm leading a church, parenting my children, heading up an international organization, or talking with a friend, my vision of God inspires me to make missionaries wherever I am and however things are going.

Revelation matures us, and so a pioneer, changed by revelation, receives something the world is searching for . . .

Authenticity.

Questions for the pioneer

1. Please list your most awkward question for God and your most awkward question for yourself.

2. What captured your attention? What was your burning bush experience?

3. If vision comes through a conversation of awkward questions, in what practical ways can you keep that conversation going? Don't just think, *What different questions do I have?* Think, *What different ways can I ask those questions?*

REVELATION | Your Story

Loner

Revelation #1: *People will believe in you, but they do not believe in 'it.'*

Don't be confused by it. Don't be concerned by it. Don't be crippled by it.

Just before Jesus hit the teenage years, He hit the first test of a pioneer.

> *"Why were you searching for me?" he asked. "Didn't you know I had to be in my Father's house?" But they did not understand what he was saying to them.*[23]

During the stage of revelation, the test you will face as a pioneer is the one of being a loner. At this stage, people believe in *you*, but they may not believe in your vision. In fact, when you share your idea, please do not be surprised if those closest to you do not understand it. They may grasp aspects of your vision, but the things that make it unique will be the things that most confuse them.

It is a lonely place to be.

When I shared the vision of the Pais Project, some of my best friends, who were colleagues in ministry, totally understood the need to reach young people. They even accepted the idea that reaching into schools was possibly the best way to do this. But the two things that puzzled them about my revelation were that I would place different team members in different churches and that I would make the apprenticeships free.

The first part of this test can seem deceiving. People do believe in you. They will come around you. They will even encourage you. But those encouragements will come with warnings, and the warnings could easily put you off. These warnings are not the negativity of evil people. They are the genuine concerns of people who can see *you*, but cannot see what has been placed within you.

So what is the lesson to be learned?

Pioneers keep pioneering when their friends are more concerned about *them* than '*it*.'

Resources

Revelation #2: *People may resource you, but they may not resource 'it.'*

Count on it. Budget for it. Believe for it.

The second part of this test is a product of the first part of the test.

People may give to your needs, but they may not give to the needs of your vision.

I found at this stage that people, out of sheer love and concern for me, would finance me personally or support me in whatever way they could. The problem with this was that I could not grow the vision based on resources I received. I could simply survive.

The lesson here is very simple. At this first stage, people resource you, but pioneers resource '*it*.'

I want to be really honest with you; if you have a vision, it's going to cost you. More than likely, you personally will have to sponsor your vision in its initial stages. The Foxy Lynn[24] and I paid for the first two years of Pais out of money that was meant to keep us in food and shelter.

I met a friend of mine, Kevin Pimblott, at a motorway service station in the middle of the UK. Kevin had many contacts throughout the country, and I was trying to recruit my first few team members. I spent about an hour sharing my idea with him, and he agreed to promote the opportunity wherever he went. As we were wrapping up, he looked a bit puzzled and asked, "Is that it? Is that all you wanted to know?"

"Yes," I replied.

"But don't you want to know about the money?" he inquired.

He went on to explain that the 46th richest man in Britain had given him scholarships to subsidize low income schools workers. The conditions were simply that the money would go toward monthly bills and maybe a vacation in the summer.

I took that scholarship money, and after several conversations with Kevin where I asked, pleaded, and tried to charm him, it was agreed I could use the money to set up Pais.

For seventeen years, Pais was technically my hobby.

During this time, I worked for three churches and in each case was paid for a position within the church. All three of those churches released me in the vision to differing degrees. The first encouraged me, the second allowed me, and the third supported me for the primary purpose of its impact within that particular church. The drive, however, to push Pais beyond into other cities and nations was not something external, but internal.

When a pioneer's vision comes from that seed planted by God, it needs time to take root. Perhaps this is why there are fewer pioneers for the Kingdom than there should be. You are far more likely to receive funding or a salary to execute an already-proven method or activity, even if that method or activity is no longer working very well. To love not only God, but also His dream of advancing the Kingdom, you will have to make choices. But let me encourage you with this:

It is better to have pioneered and lost funding than never to have pioneered at all.

Beggar

Revelation #3: *No one will ask you to do it.*

Don't doubt it. Don't demand it. Don't be delayed by it.

The purest vision does not come to the pioneer secondhand.

Bartimaeus was blind; he was also a beggar. Yet he was unlike the many other beggars on that road [25] in that his revelation of Jesus as 'the Son of David' was given to him by God. This is clear because his statement was the first public acknowledgment of Jesus' messiahship recorded in the Bible. [26]

For some, however, like more usual beggars, vision comes from scraps cast away by others. They live off the revelation of a leader or a preacher or a place they visited. They grab an idea from here and one from there, ignoring or sidestepping the awkward conversation.

Pioneers do learn from other visionaries. We benefit from their advice and even from aspects of their models and programs. But we must never skip the process.

Why?

It is simple. No one will show you the thing that only you can see.

No church ever asked me to start the Pais Project. Nobody hired me to do it. Nobody paid me to do it. Nobody even suggested it.

My church gave me contacts and encouraged me to serve the Kingdom. They gave me generic youth work to do, but I went off the end of the map I was given by others, and my journey took me to unexplored places.

Importantly, my vision did not replace my job description . . . It was simply a better way to fulfill it.

Barbados

Revelation #4: *It does not need to hurt.*

It can be joyful. It can be fruitful. It can be hopeful.

Pioneering can grow you in such a way that you may rarely notice the growing pains.

I love to surf, and so on the tenth anniversary of the Pais Project, an offering was taken to give our family a month long sabbatical. I bought my second favorite book, *The Stormrider's Guide to the 80 Greatest Surf Spots in the World.*[27]

I tend to get obsessed with things, and so for about three weeks, I read the book inside and out, coming to the conclusion that Barbados was the best place to go at that time of year. I absorbed every little fact I could. I knew the name of every single wave spot and if it was a beach break, reef break, or point break. I knew if the wave went left or right or both ways. I did not just *look* at the surfer on the front cover; I *was* the surfer on the front cover!

Next, I went to the gym to get my body ready for my dream trip. On the first day, I set the treadmill for a fifteen-minute hill run, pressing the button so that the ramp rose to a thirty-degree angle. Within about two minutes, I was gasping for air and counting down the time I had left. At the gym I attended, the television screens in front of the machines were often tuned to some dull sitcom or Oprah interviewing a man who had a sex change and was now called Brenda and was going to have a makeover and meet her long lost son flown in from Australia. On one particular day, however, a TV screen about twenty feet to my right showed a surfing expedition. After five minutes of physical torture, I unplugged my ear phones, relocated to the machine in front of the screen, and set my fifteen-minute program.

The show was fantastic! It was a documentary of five surfers who had toured Indonesia's best surfing spots. I got so into it that at one point, the surfer went left and so did I, falling off the machine with a crash. Embarrassed, I got back on and continued to run. Then the worst thing imaginable happened—my machine broke. Or, so I thought. When I looked down, it was flashing 'fifteen minutes.'

I had run the race but had not noticed the effort.

That is what vision does for us. When we lose vision, we notice the pain. It might be the pain of sacrifice, the pain of self-image, or the pain of self-doubt, but we notice the pain.

The lesson? Always keep the vision in front of you.

That sounds cliché, because it is. Yet it's still true. So how do you do it? By taking the phrase and making it literal in your life. Put up pictures, keep thank you letters, post videos on your Facebook timeline.

Do anything you can to keep your mind on the fruit, not the fight.

F1

Revelation #5: *It requires you to see the invisible driving line.*

Imagine it. Be inspired by it. Inspire others with it.

The first stage of pioneering is just that . . . the first stage.

Your ability to move forward with speed and without stalling will have less to do with your resources and more to do with your resourcefulness. It will come from something you find that others have yet to discover.

Damon Hill, the British Formula One champion from the 1990s, was once asked how he could drive around corners at such high speeds without hitting the curb. He replied, "It's simple. Don't look at the curb. Look for the invisible, imaginary driving line."[28]

When I was younger, my favorite computer game was a Formula One simulation. It had various settings of difficulty. The easy setting did not make the car go faster or the other cars go slower. It simply added a white dotted driving line. Hill is right, the minute you take your eye off the vision and concentrate on avoiding the curb, you either hit it or steer so far away to avoid it that you hit the opposite curb.

The Pharisees had a similar problem. They focused on not sinning and hit the curb of legalism that blinded them to a visit from God.

The best way to avoid potential disasters is to stick to the purest driving line. The spectators will watch—some may find it hard to look—expecting you to crash any moment. But if you keep going, if you stick to it, then it will start to become visible to them.

If you can imagine it, eventually others will too.

Questions for the pioneer

1. What is your *'it'*?

2. Are people displaying a belief in you but not *'it'*? If so, how are they doing this?

3. What are some ways to keep your vision in front of you?

REVOLUTION

STAGE TWO

REVOLUTION | My Story

Net

Around the time the first Pais team was launched, I was reading the account of Jesus getting into the boat of His new friends.

> When he had finished speaking, he said to Simon, "Put out into deep water, and let down the nets for a catch."
>
> Simon answered, "Master, we've worked hard all night and haven't caught anything. But because you say so, I will let down the nets."
>
> When they had done so, they caught such a large number of fish that their nets began to break. So they signaled their partners in the other boat to come and help them, and they came and filled both boats so full that they began to sink.[29]

A question suddenly popped into my mind.

> Paul, if you were one of the disciples and you knew a week before that this was going to happen, what would you do?

Think about that. What would your answer be?

The answer came to me a split second after the question:

> I would spend the entire week building a bigger net.

If the disciples could only catch as many fish as the net could hold, then certainly building a bigger net meant catching more fish. Investing my time in creating a bigger net rather than spending each day catching just a few fish was obviously the most effective thing to do. Making missionaries rather than simply *being* a missionary was clearly the best way for me to help advance the Kingdom of God.

And then I heard one more thing, not so much a question, more a command:

> *Go do it then.*

But how do you weave a net?

Joe, a pastor in Manchester, was the first person to ask for a Pais apprentice. His initial requirements were a male, twenty-one years old or over, with a year's experience in ministry. I managed to recruit someone who fit the bill, but Joe decided that the applicant did not fit the church. Eventually they accepted Lisa, an eighteen-year-old high school graduate with no experience and anatomically opposite of the required gender.

Lisa had been in a relationship with her boyfriend since they were both fourteen years old, and it was a real sacrifice for her to move from Staffordshire in the middle of the country up to Manchester. But she did it. She was an excellent team member and in the second year of Pais, she became a team leader. Along with Gary who became the other team leader, we created two teams reaching twice as many schools.

Pais grew from five on one team, to two teams of four and myself.

Toward the end of her second year, Lisa began to think of home, her school, her teachers, the young people of Staffordshire, and of course her boyfriend.[30]

And so more questions occurred to us.

Could we put Pais in another city? Could we plant it in Lisa's hometown? Did her hometown even *need* Pais?

Susan

The world is a desperate place.

If you've watched any television, you have seen terrible news about an awful tragedy, injustice, or atrocious act. For most of my life, these stories happened overseas in some distant land. This changed, however, when one evening a news reporter told the story of Susan.

Susan was a fifteen-year-old girl who had been kidnapped, held hostage, and tortured for an entire week. At the end of that time, her attackers took her a few miles away, removed her teeth to prevent identification through dental records, poured gasoline on her, and then burned her to death. Before she died, she managed to crawl to a road where a passer-by spotted her and contacted an ambulance. On her death bed, Susan told the police what had happened to her and who had done this terrible thing. Then the news program put up the pictures of the killers who were 'friends' of Susan and, inspired by the film *Child's Play*, had abused and murdered her.

As Lynn and I sat there in front of the TV, our mouths dropped opened . . .

We knew them.

Our lovely, gentle, and kind nextdoor neighbor was their grandfather. The news report then showed pictures of a large three-foot wooden spoon to which Susan had been tied while being repeatedly hurt in unmentionable ways. Lynn could not believe it; as a mobile hairdresser, she had often gone to the killers' house to cut their hair and moved the spoon off the kitchen wall in order to create space for a temporary salon.

As shocking as this was to her, what came next made me sick to my stomach. As it concluded, the report showed the house where this young girl had been held captive. It was a stone's throw from our home. During that week, I had walked by that house four times each day. To work in the morning, back for lunch, back to work in the afternoon, and returning home at the end of the day. Twenty times that week I walked past that house. Where was I going?

To my church office.

Last weekend you may have gone to your church, passing many houses, completely unaware of what was going on behind its walls. Susan was a typical British teenager. The chances of her walking into a church were something like one hundred to one.[31] The chances of the church walking into her life needed to drastically increase!

How do you weave a net?

With partnerships. With many people from many backgrounds, with different opinions and personalities . . . but with one vision:

To bring the Kingdom of God to Susans everywhere.

DNA

We don't need a new kind of *program*; we need a new kind of *person*.

If we were to plant more teams to reach more young people, then we knew the DNA of our teams would be key. Rather than investing heavily in promotion, we decided to invest heavily in people. We wanted more apprentices, the type who would pursue the Kingdom above their own personal agendas. I created a teaching series called the Kingdom Principles for just that purpose. Fully explained in another book[32] of this trilogy, all the principles are built around one premise:

> To change the world, we must make the Kingdom of God our *primary* concern.

This is the proposition that drives us.

The church I was a part of encouraged that mentality. They were less interested in fame and fortune than they were in furthering the Kingdom. Harry Letson, my pastor, encouraged the church to employ me on £50 a week, which was then around $75. Not a lot of money, but I suspected he took a dip into his personal wage to make this happen.

One day, not long after I began to help my pastor with youth and community work, Harry received a call for help from a local church. They had just held a successful one-week Bible club, resulting in more young people attending than they could properly handle. They had no youth pastor and so, despite the needs of his own youth ministry, Harry released me for an entire year to help the church minister to young people. All the while, he still paid my salary.

Selflessness is taught; I'm not convinced it's natural to us.

The selflessness of Harry and the other supporters and their genuine commitment to a dream bigger than their own are what made Pais possible. Twenty years later, now retired, Harry knows that his ministry may not have made him a popular Christian celebrity, but millions of young people have been impacted all over the world. More than simply introduced to Jesus, they have been given the chance to be discipled by thousands of Pais Apprentices who dedicated a year or more of their lives to them.

In this second stage of pioneering, gaining 'seek first' partners is crucial.

No matter how many apprentices we could recruit, Pais was never going to be enough. I realized that we were to be just one piece of the pie. I knew that Pais should never become independent. It was to become interdependent. And to do so, we needed to find partners with the same DNA.

We had a major impact on some local schools, partly due to the fact that we partnered with two other organizations. One was the World Wide Message Tribe, led by a friend of mine, Andy Hawthorne, OBE. They did phenomenal one-week concerts with an event on the Friday night. Another group was a smaller Youth for Christ team. They worked with us on some lessons, and Pais ran a weekly lunch club.

But over the years, not every group has been so keen to partner, and just because they're Christians doesn't mean they share the same DNA. This became clear to me when working at a high school very near to where I lived. It had the highest absentee rate of any school in England: 42% absences on a typical day. The students were described by one teacher as "totally visionless." So we invited another organization to come in and prepare lessons with us. Together we created a series on hope, resurrection, and Jesus, and then taught it as part of the school's Religious Education.[33]

Three or four weeks later, a young person from our church asked, "Why weren't you at the school today?"

It turned out that our partners had approached the school separately, organized a new series, but had decided not to include us. When I asked them why they had done this, they replied they did not want to perplex the administrators with too many Christian organizations approaching them. "We don't want to confuse the school," they said.

It has become a line I have heard several times since.

Chatting with the teacher, however, revealed that her principal had told her, "The more the merrier," and that having more than one organization helped guard against the accusation of allowing proselytizing by one particular church or group. I contacted my new friends who apologized, and we continued to work together. Yet this was a small insight into the new world of corporate Christianity that

I was beginning to experience. The one where we 'seek second' the Kingdom. The world where we see others as *competition* instead of *companions*.

In my journey as a pioneer, I have seen too many Christian brothers and sisters who have lost sight of why they were called.

Where did Susan go to school?

To the one we did not want to . . . "confuse."

> *When bull elephants fight, the grass always loses.*
>
> *[African proverb]*

Free

By this second stage of pioneering, a number of things had made Pais distinctive. We placed apprentices in churches of various denominations. We emphasized experiential, not just educational, discipleship. Our apprentices were not detached from sponsoring churches but were actively involved with their daily programs.

And perhaps most distinctly, Pais apprenticeships were free.

In the past, people had told me that fact alone would stop us from growing beyond a couple of teams. In fact, a good friend of mine explained that Pais would only work in Manchester because of my special relationships there. No one else would go for such a peculiar structural dynamic. I even remember one meeting where I was asked how big I thought Pais could grow; I told them that I could imagine a day when Pais might have as many as a hundred apprentices. One of my friends then told me that it could never grow beyond a dozen unless we changed our economic model. He was so convinced that he said if we grew that much without charging a fee, he would "kiss my bottom!"

Initially, I thought making Pais free would be a popular decision. I thought it would encourage people to partner with us. I presumed it would get me the platform I needed in order to recruit as many young adults as possible.

Yet, again, I was wrong.

The things that made us distinct, the things that made us unique, the things that made us effective, made us something else.

They made us threatening.

Questions for the pioneer

1. What is being presented to you as the issue? What does your gut instinct tell you the problem really is?

2. Do you feel you own the vision or it is simply being entrusted to you? What is the difference?

3. Do you view others as competition or companions? In what ways could partnering with others enlarge your vision?

REVOLUTION | Our Story

I-30

As a rabbi, Jesus would have been very aware of the rabbinic mantra:

> *Be deliberate in judgment, make many disciples, and put a fence around the Torah.*[34]

When you see the phrase 'put a fence around the Torah,' what does that mean to you?

Does it conjure up the idea of protecting God's Word? If so, you would be mistaken. The phrase actually meant something very different and refers to a common religious practice. To avoid sin, spiritual leaders would put a 'fence' around the law by adding a commandment between the sin and what their followers were allowed to do. They would restrict them from going anywhere near breaking God's law by creating a new law that would act as a buffer.

Not far from my house is Interstate 30. It has a speed limit of 60 miles per hour. For argument's sake, let's just say this represents God's law. So if I were to go above 60 miles per hour, I would be breaking His rule. Now if the Pharisees were alive today, they might say in order to not break God's law, we will create a fence around it. From now on you must not go beyond 55 miles per hour in order to protect you from breaking God's limit of 60 miles per hour.

The Pharisees saw this practice as crucial to their future because they believed that if Israel could clean up its act, then God would send the Messiah to set them free from the Romans. They were literally hedging their bet. This created all manner of problems.

Imagine for instance that a young pregnant wife goes into labor. Her husband helps her into the car and they set off on I-30 to get her to the hospital as quickly as possible. The baby appears to be in danger, therefore he drives as fast as God's law allows him—60 miles per hour. A Pharisee of Jesus' day would stop and condemn him. "How dare you break the law!" they might say.

Whose law?

Laws are good in that they help us understand if and where we are failing. But they do not have the power to help us succeed. Yet we, as well as the Pharisees, sometimes behave as if they do.

We live on a line defined by *do's* and *don'ts*. We create systems and then hope that we can rely on that structure to move us forward. We re-act to the system rather than pro-act on the Spirit's moving. Jesus understood something all pioneers need to realize:

Systems should be our servants; we should not become their slaves.

> Going on from that place, he went into their synagogue, and a man with a shriveled hand was there. Looking for a reason to accuse Jesus, they asked him, "Is it lawful to heal on the Sabbath?"
>
> He said to them, "If any of you has a sheep and it falls into a pit on the Sabbath, will you not take hold of it and lift it out? How much more valuable is a man than a sheep! Therefore it is lawful to do good on the Sabbath."
>
> Then he said to the man, "Stretch out your hand." So he stretched it out and it was completely restored, just as sound

as the other. But the Pharisees went out and plotted how they might kill Jesus.[35]

Jesus put humanity before hedges.

In doing so, He experienced this second stage of revolution. The stage where what we do to further the Kingdom must break the invisible laws. The stage where going the extra mile brings us into conflict with those who benefit from the first mile.

B'reishit

During the first stage, others may have seen you as a dreamer, harm-less and naïve, but at this stage, the seed of that dream begins to sprout and take root. It starts to grow.

To others' amazement, it actually works!

Now for some, this means they are more likely to get behind you. For others, however, you will find that the reverse happens. I will explain this dynamic more in the next chapter. But for now, let me unpack this second stage of pioneering by first challenging you to break out of the systems created for and by you.

Just what drives authentic breakthrough?

God is a pioneer. He tells us His story, but something tells us He's not telling us everything. For instance:

In the beginning God created the heavens and the earth.[36]

This verse tells us that God created the heavens and the earth and that He did it in the beginning.

Simple . . . or is it?

During the 11th century, a Jewish rabbi from France named Rashi highlighted the unusual wording of this verse in Hebrew. Throughout the ages, his comments have created much opportunity for discourse and debate among those who study the Torah. What the rabbi noticed was an oddity in the structure of the first word of the first verse in the first chapter of the Bible. *In the beginning.*

If the intended meaning of the word for 'in the beginning' was 'at first' or 'in-beginning,' the obvious Hebrew word used would have been *b'rishonah*. Instead God tells us His story using the word *b'reishit*, which actually means 'in-beginning-of.'

    In-beginning-of God created the heavens and the earth.

This leads to the obvious question: In the beginning of what? Exactly what was God in the beginning of when He created the heavens and the earth? A game of Monopoly? Wallpapering the living room?

Although there are many nuances, eventually the majority of rabbis came to the conclusion that He was in-beginning-of going beyond Himself. Yet how can God possibly go beyond Himself? God is omnipresent. He is everywhere.

A further understanding leads us to believe that God was creating an opportunity to pour out His love. He was in the beginning of creating *more* opportunities to love.

    God is love.[37]

God is a pioneer of love.

Kingdom pioneers are those who do not simply react with love to opportunities around them, but those who look to create opportunities to pour out God's love. Line-dwelling works against this because it is restricted at both ends by certain guidelines set up for us. Line-dwelling limits us to try new ideas, but only up until the point they clash with the system.

In this second stage of pioneering, we leave the line.

We break the rules.

Not God's rules, but our rules. Not God's rules for us, but those we have created for ourselves and those we pretend God created that are helpful for us to hide behind.

Let me suggest three examples of things from which pioneers need to break free.

Word

The first is the invisible word.

Driven by God's love for me and a love for what God wants to see happen, my 'going beyond' was reaching into schools. Since statistics show that most people who become Christians do so between the ages of four and fourteen, making Pais free in order to get more young missionaries into schools was perhaps the most impactful thing I could possibly do.[38] Yet as I mentioned before . . . no one commanded me to do it.

Too many are waiting to be given a 'word.'

We spiritualize our reluctance by claiming we are waiting for God's permission and 'peace.'

It might be the word 'go.' It may be the word 'salary.' It could be the word 'title.'

Many are bound, limited by the fact that they are waiting to be told to do something, to be given status by leading something, or to be guaranteed an award for attempting something.

Perhaps this is why there are so few pioneers. It is much easier to find a salary, a title, and praise for executing an idea or system that someone has already established . . . even if that system is no longer working.

Worker

The second is the insecure worker.

> *"Teacher,"* said John, *"we saw a man driving out demons in your name and we told him to stop, because he was not one of us."*

> *"Do not stop him,"* Jesus said. *"No one who does a miracle in my name can in the next moment say anything bad about me, for who ever is not against us is for us."*[39]

Four times the gospels record Jesus using this kind of phrase.

Twice in the negative: "If they are not for me they are against me."

And twice in the positive: "If they are not against you, they are for you."

I have heard the negative preached many times, but I cannot remember the second statement, recorded just as often, ever being taught. If Hebrews is right when it says we need to look to Jesus as a role model of pioneering, then this statement has to have huge significance in our thinking.

We tend to make two mistakes.

First, we approach the world as being against us unless it is for us; and second, what we really mean by 'for us' is 'part of us.'

At this second stage of pioneering, you will come into conflict with the corporate Christianity to which the disciples succumbed, an insecurity that needs to have the control of and the credit for Kingdom advancement.

A supportive Christian teacher once gave me an opportunity to start a lunch club in an all-boys school. Around thirty young boys attended each week, many of whom were of the Islamic faith. At one point, the teacher said to me, "Paul, if the parents of these boys find out, there could be trouble ahead." So she decided to change the time of the club to make it more difficult, therefore filtering out the least committed. So we held the club after school hours and it worked! The numbers dropped considerably to only the really interested ones . . . and every single one of them was a Muslim.

A week later, she shut the club down completely.

The biggest obstacles I have faced are Christians who believe that greater is he who is in the world than He who is in them.

World

The third is the invincible world.

As one English preacher once said:

> The world you cannot enter is the world you cannot reach.[40]

Many years ago in Britain, communities gathered together in two places. One was called a public house. Like a typical home but much bigger, public houses catered to large gatherings and contained game rooms, kitchens, and lounges. The community met at a public house for fun, relaxation, and laughter. The other place was the church. The community gathered there to learn together, worship together, and serve together.

One day the owners of the public houses decided that if people were not for them, then they were against them. They told the community, "It's us or them . . . Choose." And there was a split. No longer did those entering churches go to the pub, and no longer did those entering the pub feel comfortable to enter a church.

What is wrong with this story? It is not entirely true. It was not the owners of the public houses but the 'owners' of the churches that created the polarization.

An American parallel may possibly be the separation of Church and State. When I came to America I was told it would limit our ability to work in public schools, so I presumed that this was something the State had implemented. I was surprised to find out it was created to calm the fears of the nation's Christian founders. The first record of this phrase being used was by Thomas Jefferson who wrote to a Baptist church:

> Believing with you that religion is a matter which lies solely between Man and his God, that he owes account to none other for his faith or his worship, that the legitimate powers of government reach actions only, and not opinions, I contemplate with sovereign reverence that act of the whole American people which declared that their legislature should "make no law respecting an establishment of religion, or prohibiting the free exercise thereof," thus building a wall of separation between Church and State.[41]

I fully understand that this is a deeply complex issue, but I just want to point out that it was this imagining of a worst-case scenario that led to the situation which many Christians now think is insurmountable.

We are created in God's image so others can imagine God. We are, therefore, also given the gift of imagination.

The best use of imagination is to create new opportunities in which to be the image of God.

The worst use of imagination is to imagine the worst.

Questions for the pioneer

1. What systems need to be broken for your dream to move forward?

2. Of the three examples of things that pioneers must break free from, which do you identify with most closely? Why?

3. If love drives authentic breakthrough, describe how you can use love to authentically break through these hidden fences.

REVOLUTION | Your Story

Threat

Revolution #1: *People may believe in* you, *but are threatened by* 'it.'

Expect it. Accept it. Connect it.

Let me just rant here for a moment.

As an Englishman, I believe 'iced tea' is an oxymoron. Iced tea is simply not right. Tea is meant to be hot. If God wanted tea to be cold, we would pick tea leaves in Alaska. We pick tea leaves in India, and India is hot. It is a clue! Iced tea is just dirty water! It is yet another example of what goes wrong when man plays God.

Okay, now I've gotten that off my chest, the reason I bring this up is that the phrase 'a pioneer' is also an oxymoron.

The Encarta dictionary defines the word oxymoron as 'a phrase in which two words of contradictory meaning are used together for special effect.'

> Act naturally. Good grief. Living dead. Pretty ugly. Microsoft works.[42]

It is true that it takes one person to change the world. But, that one person can never do it alone. A pioneer's most important skill is the gift to build a team. Therefore, to see God's vision fully realized, you will need to pass the test of being seen as a threat.

At that time Jesus went through the grain fields on the Sabbath. His disciples were hungry and began to pick some heads of grain and eat them. When the Pharisees saw this, they said to him, "Look! Your disciples are doing what is unlawful on the Sabbath."[43]

This is a classic case of a group of leaders feeling threatened. The Pharisees' power was based on the premise that the oral law was as authoritative as the written law and they were the best interpreters of this oral law. Here, a number of Jesus' followers appeared to break that oral law. Immediately the Pharisees saw this Jesus, a rabbi growing in popularity, as a risk to their position. The fact that Jesus' answer was brilliant did not help . . . It just made things worse.

You see, at the Resistance Stage, people may believe in *you*, but are threatened by *'it.'*

Your success may be seen as a threat to some. They may not directly attack you, but they may try to find a way to diffuse you. They may not be able to tackle your new way head on, because now it may be making too much sense or be clearly recognized as a Biblical concept. Instead they will find other ways to dismantle what could blow their old systems sky high. For some, the old way of doing things now provides money, position, and power. Not only that, but some of them may have been the pioneers God used to open up previous ground. You need to take note of this.

Now is not the time to cast blame or shame; now is the time to engage and give them a sense of ownership. Your challenge is not to glorify yourself in a martyr complex but to help them see you are building on what they began. If you can communicate your ideas in this way, you will help some of them come with you on the journey . . . and that is important.

Because pioneering should never be about the pioneer.

Withdrawal

Revolution #2: *Don't misinterpret passive aggression as His divine direction.*

Don't read into it. Don't spiritualize it. Don't project God into it.

People threatened by *'it'* will withdraw resources.

In this second stage, the same people who might have patronized you, may now be surprised to see your plans flourish. Suddenly they take your vision a little more seriously. Now bear in mind, many will indeed be thrilled about your vision and want to get on board, but this book is intended to provide the full picture of what it means to become a pioneer. Therefore, you must recognize that as people take you more seriously, they will realize the implications of your vision to their own situation.

Making Pais apprenticeships free created a problem for me. It was intended to allow as many people as possible to train in youth and campus ministry, but initially it worked against that very idea.

I had friends, colleagues, and other companions who were themselves running internships. The problem I was giving them was that their internships cost money. Sometimes, thousands of dollars. Those fees were then used to give a salary to the person running the internship program. Pais was the first I knew of that broke that mold. Lynn and I decided to make it free and trust God to provide for us in other ways. Yet this idea caused problems for many.

"How can I give you an opportunity to get up and talk about your free apprenticeship when we will get up and talk about our more costly internship?"

Suddenly, the more Pais worked, the less opportunity I had to speak at conferences and recruit people. Sometimes, the other fishermen see you catching fish, and rather than helping you find new seas to fish in, they refuse you the use of their nets.

This has serious implications for those who find God's direction in circumstances. Those who mistakenly see a lack of resources as God shutting a door will fail at this stage of pioneering. A lack of resources is not a lack of God's hand upon you.

He is just helping you find out how much you love what He loves.

Knife

Revolution #3: *Defend 'it,' but don't defend yourself.*

Watch your words. Watch your actions. Watch your heart.

Pioneering can get very personal, because you are not executing someone else's idea. You are presenting your own revelation as an alternative, and this requires a high degree of vulnerability.

> *For our struggle is not against flesh and blood, but against the rulers, against the authorities, against the powers of this dark world and against the spiritual forces of evil in the heavenly realms.*[44]

The writer of this letter uses this word 'against' several times. The original word specifically refers to hand-to-hand battles. As I said, pioneering can get very personal; however, the personality we are really dealing with is a spiritual one.

To react humanly to a spiritual battle is tantamount to bringing a knife to a gunfight.

Although it is not primarily an emotional battle, we often engage our emotions before we engage our spirit. Although it is not primarily an intellectual battle, we often engage our minds before we engage His spirit. Instead, successfully moving through this second stage requires that we remember Jesus' often misunderstood command to turn the other cheek.

> But I tell you, do not resist an evil person. If someone strikes you on the right cheek, turn to him the other also.[45]

Although well-known, the true meaning of this statement is hidden to many of us. Notice Jesus purposely mentions the right cheek. He's emphasizing a certain type of cheek-slapping, a back-handed slap to a person's right cheek. This type of blow would result in a minor amount of pain, but was considered particularly insulting and could lead to a heavy fine, especially in a culture based around honor and shame. What's so important about that?

The illustration is less about *conflict* and more about *competition*.

The Greek word *anthistemi* is the basis of the English phrase 'not to resist,' but is more accurately and in this context best translated as 'do not compete.'[46]

We should not compete with the world *in the way* that the world competes. I have attempted to obey this command by responding in the exact opposite way of how we have occasionally been treated. Countless times over the years, great leaders with their own internships have been invited to speak at Pais conferences. Leaders, who are far more charismatic than I will ever be, have stood on the Pais platform and shared their vision. I confess that this was often a struggle. Many times when I invited others, I was concerned not because they are bad speakers, but because they are great speakers.

Jesus gives some essential advice to those He is recruiting to pioneer His Kingdom. He teaches us that before we can truly pioneer a complete path to freedom, we ourselves have to be set free from jealousy, insecurity, and in particular, the drive to justify ourselves. In the upside down Kingdom of God, winning an enemy over is considered greater than beating one.

Jesus' comment was about competition.

It is not one.

Cracks

Revolution #4: *Don't believe the lack of hype.*

You will be disrespected. You will be underrated. You will be vindicated.

There seems to be a misconception about visionaries. Others incorrectly assume that they do not see obstacles and therefore blindly pursue their dreams. Yet pioneers are totally aware of the obstacles. In fact, what sets pioneers apart is the fact that they see the obstacles before anyone else. What makes a pioneer a pioneer is the revolutionary way in which he or she sets out to overcome a problem before others even realize it's a problem in the first place!

Pioneers are not blind to the obstacles in front of them; they just see a way through them.

When people feel threatened by new ideas, they have a habit of blowing up any cracks or flaws in the plan. A direct attack is pointless at this second stage, because *'it'* is working. Therefore, indirect tactics may be used.

It won't feel under attack. It will feel undermined.

For instance, since Pais was no cost to the apprentices, many of our members who stayed long-term knew they were committing to a lifestyle that likely would have a lower income. Before long, we were even labeled with having a 'poverty mindset.' I remember being at conferences where people would jokingly pass me their leftover food and tell me to take it home to my children so they could have something to eat. I didn't mind; I knew they never meant to do this in a hurtful manner. I guess I just saw it as insecurity showing itself.

However, we did lose some people because of this. Even one or two of our leaders were drawn away in those days because being on Pais was seen as the poor cousin of other ministries. Pais is definitely not a career that will make you financially wealthy, although I am now surprised by how much God has blessed some of us. I understood and still understand that consistent pioneering will bring consistent opportunities to sacrifice. But I also firmly believe that if we seek first the Kingdom of God, He will give us all we need and sometimes some cheeky little extras.[47] Remember, Jesus often wanted to highlight the benefits of seeking first His kingdom.

It's not that I don't see the sacrifice; it's that I know God will help us overcome it.

Fortunately, being forewarned about the devil's tactics arms us against them. It was therefore helpful to me many years ago when I read a story about a CEO speaking on how to cope with criticism. He told of an architect who said:

> I can take the newest building, built by the finest builders anywhere in the world, and if you give me a camera and the ability to focus various lenses, I can make that building look like it's about to fall down because I will find five or six minor imperfections, take photos, blow them up on a big screen and convince you that the entire structure is about to topple.[48]

How can you cope with the obstacles others see?

By looking *beyond* them.

Camouflage

Revolution #5: *Think less highly of 'it' than you do of Him.*

It's not about rights. It's not about being right. It's about righteousness.

The Kingdom comes when extra miles are disclosed and when evil intentions are exposed. Jesus' ministry was all about revealing those hidden things.

> So do not be afraid of them. There is nothing concealed that will not be disclosed, or hidden that will not be made known.[49]

Jesus said and did things to stir up evil. Where He went, demons were exposed and so were the religion, laws, and systems behind which they hid.

But why?

Because the attitudes, motives, and instinct for self-preservation are often camouflaged. Evil lurks like a sniper whose goal is to blend into his surroundings by painting his skin and wearing a disguise to conceal himself. The unveiling of these hidden agendas is essential if people are to see the difference between the kingdom of self and the Kingdom of God.

Jesus the pioneer had a plan of action. It was to provoke. This forced that which was hidden to be exposed as people were forced to come out of the shadows to attack Him. The second part of Jesus' plan was to react in a Godly way.

Most observers may not be able to understand the argument between the old system and the new ideas, but they can see the attitude behind them if you do the same as Jesus did. While He was persecuted, lied about, and beaten, He kept quiet, and eventually those around Him were able to see what they could not see before . . . contrast. Jesus provoked evil into the light. Then, by being good, He exposed evil as evil and the truth became evident for all to see.

A good pioneer will not just create a new path but will also help others see the real reason why the old broken paths are still being walked on.

What can stop us from providing this extra benefit to the Kingdom?

Pride.

By default, we sometimes see ourselves as successful because we compare ourselves to those we conclude are less successful than us. When we see success through the lens of comparison, we tend to see ourselves as more effective than others. We can then be tempted to see our success as some kind of 'get out of jail free' card where we are free to treat others in the same way that they have sadly treated us.

Perhaps the best advice I can offer at this stage is this:

Always, always, always . . . compare yourself to Jesus.

Questions for the pioneer

1. If others see you as competition, what can you do to help them join you on the journey?

2. Perspective is important when others are pointing to the flaws in your vision. What are some practical ways for you to take a step back and refocus?

3. Are you taking a knife to a gun fight? If you are, what kind of blade are you trying to use? Intellect? Politics? Something else?

RESISTANCE

STAGE THREE

RESISTANCE | My Story

Tricky

At age twenty and in her third year of Pais, Lisa headed home and pioneered a Pais Project team in the West Midlands. It would be the first of many team plantings all over the UK.

As the growth of the movement picked up speed, my role slowly evolved from a solo schools worker to a team leader to a manager of several teams. I travelled up and down the country every couple of weeks, visiting Pais teams to teach, appraise, and encourage them. During the late 1990s and early 2000s, my time was spent *managing* Pais, but things were changing. We now had long-term leaders who kept an eye on day-to-day details, releasing me to move us forward.

A key part of my new role was to lead the movement from addition to multiplication.

In the mid-nineties, I received a prophetic word that God would give me "access to schools everywhere I stepped." I responded to it by walking across England as an act of faith and prayer. As I set out on my journey, I was given a short passage from Isaiah to contemplate. The middle verse goes like this:

> *Enlarge the place of your tent, stretch your tent curtains wide, do not hold back; lengthen your cords, strengthen your stakes.*[50]

The tension between *enlarging* and *strengthening* is tricky.

A common mistake can be to concentrate purely on 'getting things right,' but this hinders momentum which is essential to vision. After all, a movement by its very nature has to *move*. However, the other extreme of aggressively and exclusively 'getting us out there' can lead to overreaching that causes a structural implosion or an ideological sell-out.

Isaiah was forewarning me and consequently forearming me.

We needed to advance the movement by creating opportunities to reach more people, but at the same time strengthen the movement by getting better at what God called us to do.

So how could I enlarge the place of our tent without ripping up the very tent poles that made us who we were? This is the big question that all pioneers will eventually face. The third stage of resistance first requires an understanding of exactly who and what God called you to be, as well as the ability to know what *is* and what is *not* important to your calling.

Let me explain.

Faithworks

The more successful Pais appeared to be in our ministry to schools, the more frustrated I personally became about a lack of impact. Pais is merely a means to an end; my vision is to make missionaries, not simply to run programs in schools. As I have said before, the way Pais works makes sense, but I was haunted by the question: *Is putting teams into schools enough?*

And so, we experimented.

As my Biblical research deepened, I began to teach more and more on the roots of our faith, the early Church, and in particular Jesus' discipleship of His disciples, many of whom were in their teenage years. My study led to new theories, which led to new philosophies of ministry and new practices. Subsequently, Pais began a long journey to find churches that would allow us to break traditional systems and try new ways of teaching and training.

At my heart, I am a practitioner. I have to practice what I teach. I may not always be able to perfect what I teach, but I have to know that it genuinely works. This means that when we partner, I need space and permission to test my theories. I have also learned that those willing to give me these essential ingredients are the ones humble or passionate enough to acknowledge that what they are presently doing is either not working or not working well enough. Each of these things were granted to me in my first church.

I was very much in love with 'Sharon,' the church in which I grew up spiritually, where Pais was born, and where I was given the space I needed to grow my vision. Nonetheless, a problem surfaced: we were quickly outgrowing the church. Because our conferences could no longer fit within the facility, we needed a bigger building, but this clashed with another distinctive of Pais—our economic model.

Pais is built on partnership and stewardship. We beg, borrow, and deal before we buy anything. Ideally, we will never own a building so that we can continue investing virtually every cent into people and fuel to get those people to the right places. Due to our relationship with Sharon Church, we had not needed to raise money for bricks and mortar, but now it seemed we did.

Then one day Harry, my pastor, brought to my attention Evangel Church. He had been helping this struggling group of loyal Christians by bringing teaching and some pastoral support every week. Their premises were large for UK standards, but maintenance was a problem for this group of nineteen remaining members. The building was in poor condition, including the proverbial leaking church roof, and so they were in the process of selling it to a local restaurant chain.

When we asked the church leadership their selling price, they replied that it was around £180,000.[51] And then they turned to me and made a suggestion: they could sell it to us for their remaining mortgage payments. This, they informed me, was only £46,000.60.[52] Now, some would say this was coincidence and some might say it was God, but £46,000.60 was exactly, and to the penny, how much money we did *not* have.

So they made us a new offer. If I would lead the church, Pais would get the use of the building entirely free.

Blurred

With Harry's encouragement and blessing, Lynn and I took on the challenge, trading our leadership for a new home for Pais. The church was called Evangel, meaning good news, but it could only be good news if people knew its meaning. So we began to repurpose the church, and it started to grow in attendance. It was an opportunity to try out new ideas, and with this regeneration came a new name. To us, it was far more important for that name to resonate with those outside the building than to be understood inside.

Our vision was to impact the community, and so we renamed the church *thefaithworks*. It was a statement of intent.

We began experimenting with mission, later defining it by the tagline:

> *Beyond Attraction to Application.*

One of the first things I did after taking on my new role at the church was talk to Dave, a local policeman. I asked him, "What's the worst part of Failsworth?" He replied, "That's simple. It's Dean Street." The initial problem, he explained, was late night disruption and destruction caused by local gangs. In response, the local residents locked themselves away in their homes and avoided going out. However, the gangs then started knocking on doors and when the homeowner answered, they would walk in and order the frightened occupants upstairs. Raiding the fridge, they would then watch TV, do whatever they pleased in the house until the early hours of the morning, and leave a total mess behind. We knew immediately that we wanted to help the church help those residents. We also knew that God had clearly said to us:

Build a church with blurred edges.

For a church to truly impact its community, it has to truly be a part of it. We hoped people would not be able to see where one program finished and another one started. We hoped that no single organization would get the credit, but that the community instead would see the Kingdom come. One author correctly stated that God can do anything through a man who does not care who gets the credit,[53] so not only did this small church become the home of Pais, but we also partnered with my friend Andy and planted an 'Eden Project.' This initiative encouraged leaders and volunteers to move homes and set up small, healthy communities in the heart of difficult ones.

I sent the proposal for an Eden Project on Dean Street to the local police who responded quickly, saying they had just returned from an emergency meeting about that exact area when they found my document on their desk! Plans for a Pais/Eden partnership quickly developed. Over the next five years, people moved in and bought houses, living their not-so-normal, everyday Christian lives there.

Eventually the Eden Project in Failsworth received an award from the British government due to the radical change in the community. Where there had been derelict houses, a garden was planted, and when surveyed by the local government who asked what the garden should be named, some of the residents whose lives had been touched suggested it be called . . . 'Eden.' Although the name was ultimately rejected by the council, it symbolized to us that something of the message had taken root in the hearts of the local people.

I entered Evangel Church with theories, but I left it with convictions.

The broken system that makes converts, but not so many disciples, is the mission or church that is built entirely on an *attractional* model. Now, let me first say that I believe that churches should do 'church' really well. I believe in well-executed church services that honor God not simply through *what* is presented, but *how* it is presented. In fact, when I was a young man, it is true to say that many of us loved the Head of the Church [Christ] but were a little embarrassed by the body [Church].

Years later, however, I think it is now true to say that because of the huge emphasis on attraction, many love the Church but are embarrassed that they do not know the Head that well. A former Pais apprentice, now a senior pastor, noted that at a recent baptismal service the theme of the testimonies of those being baptized was less "since *Jesus* came into my life" and more "since the *church* came into my life."

So we believe in going beyond *attraction* to *application*.

Jesus' strategy was not to say to His followers:

> Bring your friends to Me, and I will share the gospel with them.

Instead, His general practice was to encourage them to:

> Bring Me to your friends, and I will demonstrate how you can share the gospel.

Pais apprentices spend some of their time creating great youth services and inviting the church youth to bring their friends to them. The majority of their efforts, however, are spent going into the communities of young people, both demonstrating to the youth how to share their faith and empowering them to bring a positive and spiritual impact.

We do not put the responsibility to reach our world on those we teach, without first putting the responsibility on ourselves to be role models they want to invite into *their* world.

Would you invite your pastor into your workplace?

Suitcases

For Pais to take its next steps, I had to take a next step. As more and more joined us from overseas and took Pais back to their home nations, the concept of *sparking a global movement* grew in our hearts and minds.

One day while visiting our teams in Texas, I saw a book called *The Connecting Church* by Randy Frazee. On the back was a short description of a church that really wanted to impact its community. It seemed to share similar values to Pais, and I remember thinking that it might be nice to visit that church one day.

Several months later, I received a call from a pastor. At a conference in Canada, he had met a member of Pais and wanted to see if Pais could help his Connecting Church network figure out their 'missing link' . . . schools. His name was Randy Frazee.

After much prayer and discussion, it was determined that I would repurpose the student ministry of his church in Fort Worth. So, in November 2005, five years after repurposing the church in Failsworth, Lynn and I packed all we owned into seven suitcases, boarded our sons, Joel and Levi, onto a plane, and moved to the USA.

I arrived in a world where denominationalism was still dominant. In Manchester, churches from various backgrounds worked together to reach students, but now I was in a stronger Christian culture where doctrinal differences still led to independence and competition.

I discovered an interesting paradox, however. Even though many American churches were keen to guard their distinctive beliefs, they were in fact doing the exact same thing. I walked into many churches, from Southern Baptist to Pentecostal, and what amazed me most was not that they did youth ministry so differently, but that I could not see a single difference at all! They all had the same kind of program with the same kind of schedule. They taught the same. They thought the same. The only difference was that some groups had more expensive ping pong tables.

Where was the variety?! Where were the new ideas?! Where was the creativity?! One day I came up with a simple phrase which summarized my observations:

Old thinking done really well.

It was similar thinking done on different budgets with indifferent levels of success.

Stones

In Texas, we were able to experiment with discipleship, summed up in our tagline:

Beyond Education to Experience

As new apprentices joined Pais from other nations, we noticed that each culture had some distinctive qualities. The USA apprentices usually excelled in the initial classroom setting of our three-week Foundational Training Conference. But then they would fall apart on the field, struggling to communicate their faith effectively even with young teenagers.

Why?

I found an answer in the story of David and Goliath. Before David faced Goliath, he was graciously provided with his king's own armor for protection. But there was a problem, and the issue wasn't what many of us think it was. Sunday school usually paints a picture of a little David in a big boy's armor, giving the impression that the armor was physically too large for him. The real issue for David, however, is only brought to light when we understand the original words used. In essence, David turned to Saul and said:

I cannot wear this armor because I have not proven it.[54]

And for this reason alone, David discarded it.

Similarly, when many students in the USA leave their church environment, they discard the faith of those older than them because they have not proven it. David, however, was able to reach for something he had proven . . . five smooth stones. With these, he told Saul, *"Your servant has killed both the lion and the bear."*[55]

Yet we the Church, we their parents, we the system have protected our youth from every wild animal we possibly can and, therefore, denied them the opportunity to authenticate their faith. Is it surprising then that, when American students reach college, 82% of them stop attending church within their first year?[56]

The Jews in the days of Jesus had a similar idea for youth ministry. Their aim was to take young people and *'Stuff them with Torah like an ox.'*[57] The problem? Torah means way, and yet when the Way, Truth, and Life appeared, they didn't recognize Him. Yet still we think that simply filling them with Bible verses will do the trick.

In the alternative thinking of Pais, we determined to create a youth ministry built on the idea of *proving* not *protecting*.

Speaking at conferences, seminaries, or Bible colleges, I often pose the question, "When did the disciples first become Christians?" Typically, I receive six answers ranging from "when they first followed Him" to "the day of Pentecost." The answer of course is . . . we don't really know.

But then I ask, "When did Jesus first start to disciple the disciples?" To this, I receive the unanimous answer:

"When they first followed Him."

Simple logic teaches us that Jesus discipled many of His followers *before* they became Christians.[58] So why are many of our church programs set up to do the exact opposite?

In Texas, we swapped out an antiquated idea of classroom-based Bible study where presentations were made increasingly entertaining to try and conjure up students' interest. Instead we created an academy where students, led by Pais apprentices and volunteers, went into the community to experience their faith. We ran weekly activities in local neighborhoods using sport, cooking, music, etc. We rented community rooms in apartment blocks and prayed for any sick that wanted prayer. In every case, students would be given opportunities to exercise their faith. The results were amazing! Now students would pester *us* for answers! Why did this one get healed and that one not? Why did you respond that way to ridicule and this way to appreciation? Why? Why? Why?

Our experience in Texas developed over the years and led to a new form of organizational structure based on discipleship that we now call the *Talmidim Flow*. Our constant questioning of our own vision was leading us to consistently review our own answers.

Our ideas on mission, discipleship, and eventually Bible study[59] were changing and beginning to influence those who heard about them.

By default, a pioneer's uniqueness resists doing things the way they have been done before. We were beginning to tinker, not only with training the children of strangers, but with the children of church parents. And when you tinker, you tend to attract attention . . . which then brings you face to face with the third test.

Questions for the pioneer

1. What is distinctive about my *'it'*? How does my *'it'* make you feel?

2. What is distinctive about your *'it'*? How might your *'it'* make others feel?

3. What is there about your *'it'* that is not up for discussion?

RESISTANCE | Our Story

Normal

It is nice to be attractive.

People tend to pay attention to you and listen to what you say. In the past, you may have been seen as a bit of an oddball with some cute but naive ideas. If those ideas took root, they were seen as an anomaly, only working because of some explainable extraordinary circumstances. But now those ideas are spreading; you are beginning to look almost . . . normal.

And people like normal.

Normal people do normal things. Normal people are afraid of normal fears. Normal people are motivated by normal rewards. Normal people want what everyone else normally wants.

> *After the people saw the miraculous sign that Jesus did, they began to say, "Surely this is the Prophet who is to come into the world." Jesus, knowing that they intended to come and make him king by force, withdrew again to a mountain by himself.*[60]

The third stage of pioneering is resistance.

At first, you faced opposition from those who did not understand your vision. Later, they felt threatened by it. Now, however, they are faced with the realization that it is here to stay. Their minds are changing; they may even find your alternative vision desirable!

So, rather than withdrawing the resources you need, the very opposite happens:

> Again, the devil took him to a very high mountain and showed him all the kingdoms of the world and their splendor. "All this I will give you," he said, "if you will bow down and worship me."[61]

Before I explain the significance of this episode in Jesus' story, let me ask you a question:

Why did Jesus teach us one thing but do another?

He commanded us to pray that God would not to lead us into temptation. Yet He allowed the Spirit and then the devil to lead Him there. What's going on here?

The key is found in the contradiction.[62] In Luke, the order of Jesus' temptations are different from Matthew's account. Both start with the same temptation but then mix up the other two.

Why?

Firstly, we must understand that ancient writers valued the meaning of events over their chronological order. Matthew's gospel, using various hints, focuses on Jesus as the fulfillment of the Old Testament. In the other account, however, Luke unpacks the temptation story as an example of his entire book, as usual using its context within history and geography to get his point across.

The gospel of Luke intends to show how Jesus moved towards Jerusalem, invading Satan's territory and freeing those who were bound. So, in his retelling, he cuts and pastes the story to point out its significance.

Jesus is tempted in the wilderness.

Jesus is tempted in the mountains around Jerusalem.

Jesus is tempted in the very epicenter of Jerusalem.

Luke is emphasizing Jesus' progressive invasion of the devil's territory. That is one of the reasons Jesus allows Himself to be taken through these tests. He is displaying the journey of a pioneer. He is helping us understand that when a pioneer invades someone else's territory, the territory holders can react the same way as the devil. Failing to stop us by persecution, patronization, or passive aggression, they resort to another technique. More subtle, but equally destructive.

At this stage, someone may offer to *purchase* your *'it'*!

You have probably heard the expression, "If you can't beat them, join them." Well if you pioneer, then one day those around you may think to themselves, "If we can't beat them, let's get them to join us."

On the mountain, when tempted by the devil, Jesus was offered everything He knew would ultimately come, but in the form of a shortcut. You may also be presented with the opportunity to compromise in order to gain the resources needed to advance your vision. Compromise, however, often a good thing, is yet again a tricky business.

> Compromise: A settlement of a dispute in which two or more sides agree to accept less than they originally wanted.[63]

Later I will share with you the key to good and bad compromise.

For now, let me unpack the temptation of this third level and encourage you to value its remedy: the most important character trait a pioneer can have.

Details

One day a ministry with its own internship program approached me, requesting I become its next National Director. Rather than seeing Pais as competition like they previously had, they now wanted to join forces.

Initially, this appeared to be a fantastic opportunity with an organization I greatly admired. It had a good-sized platform, annually running several conferences and networking many youth leaders across the country. Our recruitment efforts would inevitably take a giant step forward. They also promised a salary, something Pais was unable to provide for me at that time and for many years later. I was excited! This looked like the obvious next step.

But as the saying goes, "the devil is in the details."

As our conversation progressed, the proposal's conditions were unraveled. Most were perfectly fine. However, one stipulated that although I would still be able to run Pais, with these two different styles of courses now under one umbrella, Pais would be required to charge its apprentices the same amount as those signing up to our 'sister' organization.

I am willing to change many things about Pais, as the need for change is constantly with us. But one thing I knew then and still know for sure is that the Pais apprenticeship should be free for those who join the movement. On this particular matter, we were uncompromising.

Ultimately, the organization and I decided that Pais staying free would not provide a workable partnership. The proposal was amicably dismissed, but a closer connection was made between the two organizations and we worked together on various projects.

It was a tough decision for me to make. We can make bad compromises for various reasons: money, influence, comfort, but the most powerful temptation is to finally grasp the thing that has previously eluded us . . .

Legitimacy.

Promotion

Recognition is a powerful carrot on the end of a crooked stick.

Earlier I told the story of the church I led in Manchester. If you remember, I agreed to lead the church so that Pais could use its building and we could model a fellowship of making missionaries. As part of my denomination's practice, I had an induction ceremony whereby I was officially ordained as the minister. Various friends, family members, and local leaders gathered with the very small congregation of nineteen adult believers. Many of those present were connected with the Pais Project, which at that time was reaching over 200,000 students in the schools of England.

On that day, an incident occurred which, although in no way dramatic, disturbed me.

I will always remember walking through the door into the main meeting area where people turned to greet me and smile. An older lady, who had been a supporter of Pais and followed its progress for some time, walked up to me. She was aware of the impact we were having in the local schools, and truly no one else in the room wanted to encourage me more. As she approached, she laid her hand on my arm and looked into my eyes. Then she uttered words that would occupy my mind throughout the duration of the entire ceremony: "Paul, I always knew that someday you would be promoted!"

What?!

How could it be that in her mind, looking after nineteen adults who were already Christians was a promotion from reaching 200,000 students, 99% of which had never been given an opportunity to respond to the gospel?

Status.

The answer is simple—she had been taught the importance of a title her entire Christian life, not directly through Christian teaching but indirectly through Christian culture . . . because where money is spent, value is added.

As a pioneer, you must resist the temptation to compromise in order to be recognized.

Recognition comes with resources. Therefore resources become a highly desired commodity for pioneers, not only because they help our vision, but significantly because we feel somehow they also validate it.

So what is the most important character trait of a pioneer?

Faith.

Provision

Rather than grasping the shortcuts to provision that will weaken their vision, pioneers need faith to wait for God to provide. But this is difficult because God provides in mysterious ways.

When Lynn and I were married, we moved into an area near Sharon Church. The neighborhood that surrounded us was difficult and rough, so much so that a national newspaper report dubbed it "a ghetto of underprivileged underachievers." [64] That did wonders for the house prices.

Over a period of five years there, the area became more violent. I constantly broke up fights and on several occasions brought bloodied people into our home to bandage their wounds. Because of our low income and my complete lack of handyman skills, our house had deteriorated drastically. Mold clung to the walls and ice formed on the inside of the windows in winter. We had no proper heating, no double glazing (double-paned windows), and no alarm system.

To cap it all, one night a bad storm blew several roof tiles off of our house. Our insurance company informed us they would not provide coverage, because it was normal wear and tear. We would need around £2000 to fix the problem.[65]

Several friends encouraged us not to continue with Pais, suggesting opportunities for well-paid positions at local churches. With a simple phone call it seemed, I could strike a deal with another party where we would both get less than what we originally hoped: I would be doing something *similar* to what God had told me, and they would hire an enthusiastic, but ultimately frustrated, staff member. Knowing that Pais was the way I could most powerfully advance the Kingdom, I declined those opportunities.

And so, we prayed. I later found out that Lynn even took it upon herself to lay her hands on the walls of our house and pray for healing.

Earlier in the book, I told you of the tragic murder of Susan, the teenage girl living nearby us. During the investigation, the police set up a mobile unit. The heavy police presence over the following weeks caused those involved in criminal activity to move out. Within the space of two weeks, one third of the residents in that small area moved away. In an attempt to keep what the local authorities called the 'respectable residents,' they found some European money to pour into the community.

A couple of days after we had prayed for provision to fix our roof, a community worker turned up on our doorstep. He informed us we could get some help to re-roof and a grant for an alarm system. What he said next, however, was particularly interesting. He told us that one street away, residents were receiving grants of up to £12,000.[66] Our neighbors would have to pay 10% towards the costs, but these grants were given in order to raise the standard of living in the community. Unfortunately, we were also informed that our house lay just outside the boundaries for those grants.

We prayed again.

Two weeks later, the local government announced that the boundaries had moved and we were now inside the eligible area. To cut a long story short, they told us after an inspection that they could give us £16,000 to help with damp-proofing and other necessities.[67] Then, after means-testing us and appraising exactly how much could be provided in grant funds . . . they told us we would not have to contribute one penny!

As work was done, more issues arose and then, due to some poor decision-making on their part, they decided to knock the entire house down and rebuild it from scratch. Our home was totally redesigned. The new plan got rid of the mold, installed central heating and double glazed windows, and, believe it or not, added an extra bedroom. Eventually they spent £62,000.[68] The only original structures remaining were one wall and the floor. Unfortunately, they could not fit in the Jacuzzi I had most politely requested.

> So do not worry, saying, 'What shall we eat?' or 'What shall we drink?' or 'What shall we wear?'[69]

Faith is not believing that God can provide; it is no longer dictating how He does it.

Storm

Some strive for quality above quantity; others target quantity before quality. However, I believe the quest of a pioneer is for *purity*. Purity leads to quality; quality then leads to quantity. Pioneers need faith to trust that if they pursue what God said, then He will provide later what the wrong kind of compromise might provide now.

When it became clear to me that I should fully launch myself into Pais, I worked out a plan with the Texas church that employed me, and we agreed on a long-term transition out of my role. After seventeen years, I was to go full-time for Pais.

Only one hindrance stood in the way. My 'tent-making ministry' had always been to work for a church.[70] It was how I funded myself to lead Pais which, because of its economic model, had no salary to give me. Yet still, I handed in my resignation and made it known that I would be giving myself completely to the movement.

One day, a few weeks before my salary from the church ended, I was speaking in Colorado. Privately, as many people in my position do, I had hoped for a large attendance at church that day. More people mean a better chance to find one or two who may catch the vision of Pais and therefore be led to support us financially.

In spite of my hope, a huge blizzard hit the area, and as I looked around the church that morning, I was greatly disheartened. Their usual gathering of almost a thousand people had depleted to sixty or seventy. I remember asking God the question, *If you believe in what I'm doing, why did you bring me here on this particular Sunday when no one is around?*

Even the people who were scheduled to take me to my next appointment were unable to make it through the extraordinarily bad snowstorm. However, it just so happened that another couple who lived in Steamboat Springs, the very city I was to visit next, were in Colorado Springs on a family getaway for the weekend. Despite the storm, they visited the church where I was preaching that morning, and since they were heading home to Steamboat Springs right after church, they offered to give me a ride. Otherwise, I would have been stranded.

Anyone familiar with the Rocky Mountains knows the traffic problems when a big winter storm hits. This trip, which should have taken about four hours, took eight. During this God-appointed journey, my acquaintances became friends. They told me that they had listened to various recordings of my teachings over the past months and asked why I had not written any books. I explained that the economic model of Pais meant that much of my time was given to working within a church in order to provide my salary. They then inquired what it would take for me to be released to write books and devote myself full-time to Pais. I replied that in order to operate independently, I would have to raise a salary equivalent to what I had been earning from the church. Nothing more was said.

On the drive, we learned that an unexpected situation arose with my planned hosts which made it problematic for them to house me. Yet another disaster! So graciously, my traveling companions offered their basement apartment for the week. I was pretty busy over the next few days and saw very little of my new friends, so they asked if we could have dinner together. During that meal, the thing you only ever read about in books happened.

They offered to fund my entire salary!

For about ten minutes I was in a daze, not fully understanding what they were saying. I had sat down to an appetizer with not a single cent previously pledged towards going full-time for Pais, but I walked away from dessert with the entire amount.

Pioneer, God will provide in many different ways, none of which you will expect.

In the last fifteen years, I have had the pleasure of meeting and getting to know some wealthy people, but this couple would not have fallen into that category. What they were giving was far more than a tithe.[71] It was their life savings. It was a sacrifice to the Lord which would undoubtedly cause a serious dent in their family's finances. They had gone the financial extra mile.

It turned out that my new patrons were also pioneers.

Questions for the pioneer

1. If compromise is *'a settlement of a dispute in which two or more sides agree to accept less than they originally wanted'* are you being tempted to settle for less than you originally wanted?

2. Write a list of strange incidents where what you needed has been provided. What does this list teach you?

3. You have one million dollars. You want to invest it where it will do the most good. Would you invest it in you?

RESISTANCE | Your Story

EasyJet

Resistance #1: *Define Yourself!*

Don't do it too soon. Don't do it too late. But do it before others do it for you.

The test of resistance is the temptation to conform. And only those who learn to define themselves will pass through this test. Let me explain why.

As Pais developed in other nations, I began to make more transatlantic flights which resulted in me becoming, I confess, a plane snob. When booking flights, I now consider the particular airline offering the trip. The lowest price is still my priority, and I have only ever travelled in economy. Yet I prefer to travel with certain airlines. Some airlines have better service. Some have little televisions that play looping movies in the back of the seat in front of you.

Others go the extra mile, offering multiple movies, plus the ability to pause, rewind, and fast forward. The choice of snacks varies as well. I know which airlines provide my favorite English delights free of charge: chunky Kit Kats, Cornish pasties, and English breakfasts. Even the quality of the little travel packs they give you can make my day. My favorite airline gives me a free toothbrush and woolly socks!

However, one Saturday night several years ago, I was traveling from Manchester to Belfast in Northern Ireland. Booking a quick flight on a no-frills airline called EasyJet, I flew out of Liverpool accompanied by a huge army of Irish Manchester United fans who had just come from a big match. The atmosphere in the airport was chaotic. A gang even tried to start a fight with me. However, the most extraordinary thing on that flight was the 'welcome' by the flight attendant who tried to communicate amidst a roar of football chants, expletives, and general pandemonium. I cannot recall her precise words but this was almost exactly what she said:

> *Listen, you lot!* We've already contacted the Belfast police. If you give me any trouble, I'll have you locked away! Don't touch me. Don't speak to me . . .

With a few quick points to the back and the side (indicating, I believe, the exits), she concluded her motivational speech:

> . . . *Now shut up and belt up!*

I just sat there. I would have liked to have gone to the restroom, but I couldn't take the risk.

Then I noticed something strange. I was in no way disappointed. There were no TVs or travel packs, and I had to pay for my chunky Kit Kat. But still, I was completely content.

Why?

Because this particular airline had clearly *defined* itself.

It promised only two things—to be cheap, which it was, and to get me there on time, which it did. EasyJet's brand was clear and simple: We aim to be the cheapest and most reliable, but don't expect frills.

Pioneers need to understand the two benefits of definition. Firstly, it tells people what they *should not* expect from you. Secondly, it holds you accountable for what they *should* expect from you. Both are very helpful.

Clearly defining ourselves releases us from unrealistic pressure to spend time on things that distract us from our main purpose. It also keeps us on track as we find ourselves not only in uncharted territory, but in unstructured territory. Hidden danger lies in the fact that we often create our own schedules, decide our programs, and initiate them ourselves.

I was around thirty-five years old when I came to the understanding of who I am. I'm not talking about my identity in Christ, but my God-given purpose and mission in life. Simply stated: *I make missionaries.*

This frees me!

When I was asked to lead what became thefaithworks church in England, I clearly communicated my theme to them. I would not be leading the church as a pastor, therefore I would not spend a great deal of time visiting people to talk about their aches and pains. Someone needed to, of course, but we would train others to do this. I would lead by making missionaries. I would invest heavily in those leaning forward, not in those drifting away.

It is a wonderful feeling when you are released to be who you are.

Notice I do not say when you are released to do what you want to do. All pioneers have to roll up their sleeves and get involved. In the early stages of pioneering, we have to do almost everything![72] But definition will eventually allow good delegation and free us to deliver on what we promised.

With that in mind, the church also was able to hold me accountable for the things I said I would bring. Empowerment. Inspiration. Mentoring. Coaching. The fruit they would see, I told them, would be a church that was active in the community. Our vision was to create a group of God's people that would be such good news to their neighbors that, if for any reason we disbanded, those in the local community would wave banners and walk along the streets protesting, *"Save Our Church!"*

Flags

Resistance #2: *Know how to compromise.*

Tell your story. Learn your history. Teach your backstory.

Definition itself will not help you in this third stage of pioneering, but it enables you to do what will—choose the right kind of compromise.

I am one of those men who have that inward drive to stick flags in maps. I even have a computer game on my laptop called Total War. I play it mostly in airports waiting for my next flight, and the incredible boredom of a delay is diminished as I slowly watch the world map turn red as my empire grows.

Am I alone? I don't think so; in fact I think my tendency is less a primeval urge and more a promoted urgency from God.

> God blessed them and said to them, "Be fruitful and increase in number; fill the earth and subdue it. Rule over the fish in the sea and the birds in the sky and over every living creature that moves on the ground."[73]

This of course has its problems.

How can you expand a vision but keep it great? How can you make partnerships but keep your vision pure? How do you build His Kingdom and not your empire? In this stage at least, those questions can hinge on a more specific question:

> *How do you determine what to compromise and what to never surrender?*

Here is a principle I use as a litmus test:

You can compromise on almost everything, except that which made your vision unique in the first place!

It has become apparent to me that Pais could flourish at a tremendous rate and receive resources I could never dream of if we simply get into the business of providing cheap labor to churches. If the vision was to provide communities with nice young people who were enthusiastic, then my life would be simpler and our reputation far bigger.

But it is not.

Pais has three unique distinctives:

Mission: to go beyond *attraction* to *application*.

Discipleship: to go beyond *education* to *experience*.

Study: to go beyond *curriculum* to *culture*.

And so, we have had to commit ourselves to those awkward conversations with churches who would give us the world if we simply provided interns. Interns are those with little training and no agenda. Our apprentices, however, are constantly being trained and come with an agenda—to be missionaries making missionaries.

So can I encourage you also to ask yourself what is more important—flags in maps that increase your fame or awkward questions that will increase your Kingdom influence?

Bungee

Resistance #3: *Establish new measurements of success.*

It is important. It is inspiring. It is inclusive.

New vision requires new measurements of success.

I know of a church whose teaching, vision statement, and structure express their heartfelt desire to touch their community. They have clearly defined themselves and often communicate this desire to their staff. They genuinely want to affect and infect their neighborhoods.

Unfortunately, it will never happen.

At least not to the levels that they wish it would. Why? Because once a week the staff meets to look at attendance statistics. It is a great church that executes everything they do very well. Yet this weekly snapshot of the figures concentrates almost entirely on the amount of people attending programs within the building. Even its measurement of community groups is an attendance count of those groups when they meet at the facility. So no matter how much the pastor may want to inspire the church to reach out, this measuring tape acts as an invisible bungee rope, pulling their focus back to what goes on inside the building. At the leadership meetings, attention is given to who came Sunday morning and how those numbers compare to the same Sunday the previous year. How was that change reflected in the finances? How would those finances impact the large cost of running the building?

These questions in themselves may be harmless. However, failing to measure the things they hope to see is very harmful. Remember, where money is spent, value is added, and where measurements are taken, focus is given.

If you want to pioneer a new vision, you must pioneer a new system of measurements.

Pais no longer measures converts; we measure disciples. For many years, team leaders reported how many young people had responded to some kind of altar call. Of course, 'altar calls' never existed in Jesus' time. Not until the eighteenth century, when our Christian faith became so individualized, did words such as 'personal

Savior' become popular. It was only during the 1950s that the altar call became prominent through a great evangelist.[74]

But Jesus did not say, "Go and make converts." He told us to "go and make disciples."[75]

Sometimes you cannot measure what is important without ceasing to measure what is not important. So, rather than measure converts, we measure integration. How many young people join us as we join with the whole family of God? We measure mission. How much impact are those we are taking with us having in their communities? We measure discipleship. How many are involved in authentic discipleship? And we measure study. To what extent are they being equipped to help their friends and family discover what the Bible is teaching them?

Our goals and expectations are centered on what makes us unique, not what makes for a good soundbite. We quantify our success in terms of our distinctives because doing so helps those who join us understand what is valuable to us and the Kingdom. I believe it helps all of us feel what God feels.

If you want radically different results, you will need radically different measurements.

Sometimes you have to cut the bungee.

Railroad

Resistance #4: *Don't limit your vision.*

Propagate it. Prune it. But don't pinch it.

Something like two hundred years ago, the people who shaped America were the railroad barons. They literally configured the USA by deciding where much of its infrastructure would be. They were powerful, wealthy, and highly influential. Then one day, some bright spark invented the production car and the railway barons met to decide what to do about it. The conclusion they came to was . . . nothing! As far as they were concerned they were in the railroad business.

Two hundred years later, the railroad barons are not nearly as influential, wealthy, or powerful. I wonder where would they be now had they realized they were not simply in the railroad business but the transport business?

A while back, at our annual Global Summit where our National Directors gather for a week to discuss vision, strategy, and new teaching, I put a simple question to them:

> Has schools work become our railroad?

As we thought through our history, we realized that we were not simply in the schools business or even the apprenticeship business . . . we were in the business of making missionaries. We rediscovered our theme and were no longer restricted by our target. That understanding exploded our vision.

The Pais Movement was the name we chose to define the organization, with the Pais Project being our specific arm to reach youth and schools. A new element, the Pais Collective, then grew out of a question other people asked us:

> How can we apply the three distinctives of Pais to our churches and universities?

The Pais Venture is a third element of Pais and came from some conversations I had with friends of mine who were in business. I wondered if we could help them in the same way we helped school children. What would it look like, I wondered, if we went into businesses and served them while modeling Kingdom behavior to the followers of Jesus in that community?

Pais Venture started with me going solo into my friends' companies to consult on teamwork and communication. Then through provoking questions, I gained the opportunity to carefully and appropriately present aspects of my faith.

Right now, as far as Pais Venture is concerned, I am back in 1988! Once I have learned a few more things, I will teach others and we will offer Venture teams to churches and business communities.

Defining Pais by our theme, rather than our initial target, has freed us to reach worlds we otherwise would have been unable to enter. Perhaps one day there will be other arms of Pais serving in areas such as the arts and who knows where else. It is exciting!

However, our litmus test has always been and will always be an awkward question.

Whatever is suggested, whatever the potential opportunity or benefit, we will continue to ask:

Does it make missionaries?

Questions for the pioneer

1. I make missionaries. The vision of Pais is *Missionaries Making Missionaries*. How might you succinctly and distinctly define and theme your vision in a short sentence?

2. What should people expect and not expect from you? How could you encourage and discourage them to do this?

3. What are the old measurements of success? What do the new measurements of success need to be for this new vision? What one thing makes your vision unique? This is what you must protect.

REPRODUCTION

STAGE FOUR

REPRODUCTION | My Story

Detours

Pais was founded over twenty years ago.[76]

That's twenty years of growth, but also twenty years of potential detours. So how do you keep growing but stay focused on your true calling? How do you release people but stay relevant?

If there is one thing about change I have noticed, it is this: those you lead may attempt to emulate what you teach, but they only really duplicate that which is in line with what you do.

The movement now consists of three elements: Pais Project (schools), Pais Collective (churches), and Pais Venture (businesses). We have teams in various nations on the continents of Europe, Africa, North America, Asia, and South America, with Australia to be added soon. During those twenty years, several thousand people have served for at least one year on Pais, many of them for multiple years. And my role has changed.

In the first stage of *Revelation*, vision is given to an individual not a committee.

By this fourth stage of *Reproduction*, vision is given to a community not just an individual.

As we grew, so did those working alongside me. They became more proficient in what we do, and they required more space in which to do it. In the early days of pioneering, I had all the ideas. I had all the vision. The greatest challenge was to convince others. Today much of our vision is based on the ideas of those growing up within it. Now I am the one that has to be convinced.

Once a year, I pull my National Directors together for our Global Summit, a week of fellowship and vision. We study together in the morning, and in the afternoons, we talk through and agree on our next steps for the year. One question we addressed as we started to plant Pais in new nations was what kind of organization we wanted to be as we moved forward.

We saw two extremes that could fence us in.

On one end was the idea of an authoritative legal organization where Pais would be one global non-profit or charity with centralized finances and charitable status. Our concern here was that we would build a static and slow moving institution.

On the other end, we knew we could grow very quickly if we franchised Pais.

I had seen this model in several places whereby local people with a parallel vision had set up a ministry, contacted a national organization, and asked if they could come under their umbrella. It's a quick and simple solution to grow an organization. Franchising Pais could make us look good because we would be able to pin more flags in a map, but ultimately we felt it would weaken and dilute the vision. It was quantity at the detriment of both quality and purity.

So we chose a third way.

We decided to shape the organization through what we saw as an apostolic model. This idea was purely based on relationship, respect, and connection. I would have no legal authority in most nations. However, we would work on such a strong relational bond that we would flow together in one direction. Our programs would be so interdependent that if you walked into a Pais office in Berlin, Accra, Chennai, or Manchester, it would feel like the same team.

Leadership, we decided, would come through a discipleship process.

I would model Pais where I lived and, through my mentoring academy, I would coach the National Directors one-to-one via Skype each month. Comprised of much more than simply reacting to their reports, the mentoring sessions would supply proactive training and workshops in specific areas. Through meeting online and geographically, I would empower, appraise, and continually pass on the DNA of Pais.

I would listen and observe what God was doing within us and through us, then teach what was needed to be done next.[77] A bit like Paul the apostle, I would travel to each nation teaching, advising, and asking questions because, as I have just said, in the beginning I had a revelation and others caught hold of it. Now many of us have revelations, and I have to catch hold of them.

> I will pour out my Spirit on all people. Your sons and daughters will prophesy, your old men will dream dreams, your young men will see visions.[78]

I am neither young nor old right now, but I am preparing for the future in which a vision is something you drive but a dream is something you support.

Slowly and gradually, I am beginning to realize that the extra mile I pioneered has for others become their *first* mile. My role as the founder and Global Director is therefore to encourage and create opportunities for them to pioneer our future. Of course I still have ideas too, because I can't stop asking those awkward questions.

I guess the spirit of a pioneer never dies. Unless you want it to.

My favorite stories are no longer those of our successes but of our successors, the people who have taken the original model of Pais to new places via new paths. These new pioneers have not detoured from the distinctives that made us unique, but have created unique ways of implementing them.

You can get to know many Pais Pioneers by watching the documentary inspired by this book, *The Spirit of a Pioneer* by Windward Productions.[79] You can also see them practicing the three distinctives of Pais in various parts of the world.

Mr. 'S' [Pakistan]

I like to think I have faith. Yet when we started a conversation with Mr. 'S' who asked us to train him to reach the youth leaders of Islamabad, I had doubts.[80] The idea of a Pais team in that city seemed surreal to me. Yet here is his story:

In Pakistan, evangelical Christians make up approximately 0.1% of the population. My heart burns for my country and to see my people reached for Christ, but I realized that despite all the ministry work God had me doing, the only way I was going to make a substantial impact was to train others to help me rather than trying to do so much on my own. This revelation led to my introduction with Pais and Paul Gibbs, who were actively engaged in raising up missionaries for the mission field in new ways. For one year, I left my wife and children in the capable hands of my extended family and went to America to train under Paul's leadership and the Pais Movement.

That year was well worth the sacrifice I made to come, as I received not only the knowledge of Pais' distinct approach to mission, discipleship, and study, but the practical experience of doing it. This proved invaluable when I returned to my home in Islamabad and started not only working in a couple of schools, but training future leaders to help me transform the youth of Pakistan for the sake of Christ. Since my return from America, I have trained seven other full-time team members to help me and they have also been training others. By the end of this year, I anticipate having more than twenty full-time Pais Apprentices helping me lead this transformation in my country.

On a practical level, we have started the first ever youth leadership academy in Pakistan.

Here we begin the process of training and equipping young people in the Pais approach to mission, discipleship, and study. We are using this as a launch pad to go into the rest of the country as we take these young people out and let them experience the work we are doing and the God that is empowering us to do it. All the while, we watch them be transformed in the process. Despite the heavy persecution in my country against Christians, I believe God is and will continue to do great things here. My vision is for us to have Pais teams in every major city in Pakistan and begin to see our impact go outside our borders to the surrounding countries. I know God was using me before I became involved with Pais, but since being trained, I am seeing what I previously could do in a year on my own, now being done every month. I look forward to the day when the work I may have been able to do on my own in a lifetime is being done every day because I equipped myself to equip others and God multiplied the results.

Kevin [USA]

As you read earlier, Kevin Pimblott was one of my first encouragers. It was fantastic to reconnect with him and watch him pioneer the Pais Collective. Now one of our coaches, he continues to inspire many.

My association with the Pais movement began in 1989 when I first met its founder, Paul Gibbs. Paul was a constant source of encouragement back then in the halcyon days of nation-wide youth and schools ministry in the U.K., and nothing has changed!

We reconnected again in 2010 when Paul helped my wife and me address some of our issues concerning the twenty-first century church. We needed to talk through what I later learned to be the three distinctives of the Pais Movement: mission, discipleship, and study. Out of these conversations came Saints Church-St. Louis and, more importantly, a renewed vision for the local church and her approach to these key features that were central to New Testament thought.

These discussions provoked us to not only launch a brand new church and the Pais Collective but also focused our minds on the crucial topics of leadership development, church planting, and the coaching of current and new leaders in a new but very old way of 'doing church'!

We now have a local church with small communities of people scattered across St. Louis, Missouri, where the vision is to see a group of people become a family of disciples living on God's mission of restoring their community. We are implementing discipleship, living on mission, and studying in 'haverim' together.[81] The Pais Collective is helping churches and leaders in both the UK and USA in particular; coaching has begun with local church pastors and leaders using both relational discipleship and mentoring. Our process of mentoring and discipleship is made particularly helpful by the mentoring packs developed over many years by Paul and the Pais Movement. The coaching of leaders has also been enhanced by the many combined years of experience that the Pais Movement has gained!

Since the inception of the Pais Collective, we have watched both churches and leaders take hold of the coaching tools and develop fresh faith and new ideas to intentionally rethink their approach to assimilation and mentoring of first-time guests and members. The Collective has coached leaders in the key issues of leading through change, recruitment, the stages of effective leadership, and much more.

Pete [England]

When I first met Pete, I actually prayed, *Please, Lord, don't let him apply to Pais.* Pete literally looked like Jesus, and I'm not a big fan of hippies. I am, however, very glad that he did apply and that we accepted him. Pete always carried the character of Pais, but the doors he has opened in recent years have required moving beyond his job description.

I joined Pais in the year 2000 as an eighteen-year-old, and at the age of twenty-one, I took on the role as UK Director in Training under Paul Gibbs' tutelage. For a couple of years, the enormity of the task overwhelmed and almost drowned me! Now over a decade later, I feel Pais in Great Britain is in a position of great strength.

Many people have predicted the death of the Church in the UK based on the hard evidence that young people have left the Church in huge numbers over the last few decades, but we have an opportunity to engage those young people in schools on a daily basis. The reality is that although young people may have left the Church, they are more and more open to the big questions around faith, God, and spiritual matters. And education establishments know that.

This has led to some interesting opportunities! Over the last few years, we have been invited to become an integral part of the day-to-day life in schools. For instance, we will have two Pais teams based in one school all day, every day. From 8am to 4pm each day of the week, Pais Apprentices are able to implement our approach to mission, discipleship, and study.

In this public school, they lead Haverim groups, mentor young people, and help students to discover their faith. This higher level of partnership with schools has also led to an invitation for Pais:GB to help create a Christian Ethos School in the North of England.

We will help shape the Christian ethos of this school, which we hope will be the first of many. From September 2014, every student in the school will be coached by Pais Apprentices. Pais Apprentices will have the opportunity to establish prayer spaces, engage students with the Biblical story through Haverim, help them apply their faith by serving their community, and encourage them to be a constant Christian role model in their school. As well as directly inputting into the lives of students, Pais will have an opportunity to play a greater role in the lives of staff, parents, governors, and the wider community connected to the school. This new experience will teach us a lot and hopefully be reproduced throughout the world!

Others

I love Pais pioneers!

People such as:

Tony Puckett who was the first American pastor to believe Pais could happen in the States and took a risk on my vision. Rob and Keren Johnson who then, as the next USA National Directors, helped Pais become a movement that worked in large mega-churches as well as in small rural ones.

André who pioneered our relationship with the German government so that the hundreds of Germans who serve with us around the world are mostly funded by their nation.

Junior and Mirjam, Nico and Josi, Armstrong and Christine, Mark and Beccy, and so many other couples who have thrown their joint gifts into the work of National Directors, each one of them implementing unique ideas in their own countries that others can then explore.

Ben and Gale joined in 1988 and eventually returned to Richmond, UK, where they repurposed their home church, becoming its senior pastors and then sending many young adults to Pais. After years of sending young missionaries to us, their leadership now consists almost entirely of Pais alumni and their combined length on Pais is forty-two years! Practicing many of the Pais distinctives, their church has tripled in size and, more importantly, in the impact it is having in their community. Ben is a now a zone leader for his denomination, overseeing forty other churches and sharing ideas with them.

One of my favorite stories to watch has been that of Mike Davies who served as an apprentice for many years and then filled in gaps where we needed him. I loved the process in which he discovered his theme and became our Global Training Director. Now he is coordinating the accreditation of our apprenticeships so that Pais members can gain a diploma and degree.[82] For years, the only way to have done this would have been to change our apprenticeship to a classroom-based academic-driven ministry. We would have had to compromise our vision. I love the fact that it was Mike, not me, who found a new way and then took us the extra academic mile.

Mark Riley took hold of our mission distinctive and built one of our catalytic programs to help others experience it in a tangible way. We may have helped him shape *Because You're Loved* and its three stages, but it was his idea, design, and insight that was its driving force. I now see videos and hear stories of it being implemented in communities all over the world.[83]

Ultimately, we pioneer not by passing on *control*, but by passing on *culture*.

How?

Well, each Pais nation is so committed to each other that they tithe toward a global pot to help recruit and plant the vision in new countries. This has helped us develop a training program for National Directors through Pais:Global. This visionary team contains a group of specialists in Texas where new pioneers come and learn the intricacies of Pais leadership and its 30 Fundamentals. Then after time spent with a Pais Nation, we send them to plant the movement as part of The Flow, our discipleship-based structure of leadership.

How do you grow people beyond the vision and yet keep them committed to it?

You do not *release* them . . . You *resource* them.

Questions for the pioneer

1. In what ways can you resource those who are walking their first mile as they follow you?

2. What are some ways you can pass along the *culture* of your organization rather than just passing on *control?*

3. What brings you the most delight—when you succeed or when those around you succeed?

REPRODUCTION | Our Story

Recruit

It has been said that the single most important thing about you is whatever drops into your mind when you hear the word 'God.' [84]

Why?

Because it is also said that whomever you see God as, you will become to other people.

I find that interesting because I have found it to be true in my life. I do not see God primarily as my rescuer. I don't think His ultimate goal was to die on the cross in order to redeem me. I am of course incredibly thankful that He did, but I believe His primary purpose was bigger than that.

Jesus did not come to *rescue* me; He came to *recruit* me!

He came to invite me into His Kingdom work and, through the cross, He provided a way for me to be worthy of taking Him up on the offer. So as a pioneer whose end goal is to advance His Kingdom, not build my empire, I have become a recruiter.

I believe He hopes you will become one too.

As Hebrews says, we need to follow Jesus' example. His successful recruitment campaign is evident in what took place soon after He departed.

Everyone was filled with awe, and many wonders and miraculous signs were done by the apostles. All the believers were together and had everything in common. Selling their possessions and goods, they gave to anyone as he had need. Every day they continued to meet together in the temple courts. They broke bread in their homes and ate together with glad and sincere hearts, praising God and enjoying the favor of all the people. And the Lord added to their number daily those who were being saved.[85]

The fourth stage of pioneering is reproduction.

At first, many people may have believed in you, but not in 'it.' Then perhaps a few believed in you, but were threatened by 'it.' In the third stage of pioneering, those same people may have believed in you and attempted to purchase 'it.'

But when people believe in you and *copy* 'it,' you have entered the fourth stage!

Others will now reshape what they do in order to reproduce what you are doing. The more people that follow, the broader and more well-trodden your path becomes . . . and the easier it is for even more people to follow. Your idea has gone through the stage of being viewed as an *anomaly* and graduated to the status of *adoption.*[86]

What was once an alternative path has now become a major highway.

Imitation really is the sincerest form of flattery!

Tupperware

So is that a good thing?

Is the aim to build something so big and successful that it dominates the ideological landscape? Is the idea to create a movement whereby everyone adopts your organization? Should every church and school have a Pais team? Is that the big idea? Is that the goal?

Or is there a *theme* rather than a *target* that we should aim for?

In order to understand the answer to that question, you have to grasp a paradigm first. It's a principle that occurred to me several years ago when watching a BBC news program. The big issue of the day was a group of young environmental activists who had spent months protesting the construction of a new highway, the A30, in a rural part of England. These activists looked like militaristic earth hippies. They had names like 'Stick' and 'Butterfly.'

The one I distinctly remember was called 'Swampy.' [87]

At age twenty-two, Swampy and his fellow eco-warriors dug tunnels underground and set traps for those who might try to pull them out. Incredibly, the traps were not designed to hurt their pursuers but engineered so that the protesters themselves would be buried alive! This led to a standoff, which lasted the better part of a year. I often tuned in to find out who was winning this battle of wills, and on one particular occasion, a sideline story caught my attention.

I watched as a small group of local, middle-aged, conservative English ladies were filmed during their daily lunchtime routine. These concerned surrogate mothers and grandmothers, dressed in their rural middle class attire, carried Thermos flasks and neatly packed Tupperware boxes to distribute to their new friends Swampy and company. I listened intently as the interviewer asked a selection of them why they were so committed to looking after a group of smelly, rebellious, and unkempt young people. Their answer fascinated me. It turned out that although they did not entirely agree with Swampy's methods or politics, they had been swayed by his commitment and passion. They shared how they had been previously ignorant of environmental issues but now had begun to campaign in their own more conservative style about the treatment of the surrounding area.

As I watched that interview, this is the paradigm that I began to understand:

It takes an extreme to influence the mainstream!

Extremists are on one side of the pendulum, and the mainstream may be on the opposite side. The passion of extremists and their commitment to go the extra mile swings the mainstream pendulum towards them. Those in the mainstream will rarely become as fanatical or single-minded about that one particular issue. However, they will become more than simply aware . . . They will adopt their cause.

Pais is an extreme that I believe will influence the mainstream. Our single-mindedness is a spark and a seed. It is not the intention of the Pais Project that everybody should become a schools and youth worker or even that every church should adopt a Pais team. Our hope is that, through complete commitment to our vision, we will cause the mainstream church to recognize and respond to the opportunity and potential that surrounds them, and that they would take seriously their responsibility to impact the youth of their schools and wider community, rather than just the youth of their church.

Our vision is to spark a movement whereby the saints' primary concern is to advance the Kingdom of God in their world. My hope is that those who adopt our ideas will take them further and wider than we have.

> *I tell you the truth, anyone who has faith in me will do what I have been doing. He will do even greater things than these . . .*[88]

Estimates put the number of Christians in the world at 2.1 billion.[89]

That's one third of the world's population.

What if one third of the world's population did even greater things than Jesus?

Examples

Pioneers often have a greater influence than they first expect.

Why?

Because pioneers, true pioneers, have an idea bigger than their idea.

They just don't realize it at first because they are usually busy getting on with the answers to their own awkward questions. At some point along the way, it dawns on them that what they are doing may have much bigger implications.

Perhaps the most obvious place we see this is in the area of business. A good example would be Anita Roddick who started her first cosmetics store sandwiched in between two funeral parlors, subsequently and controversially naming her business 'The Body Shop.' Pioneering new forms of ethics and fair trade in the 1970s, Roddick, like most trailblazers, started very small. Rarely does a pioneer start with big backing or even adequate resources. Her first Body Shop was on a back street away from pedestrian traffic. Roddick demonstrated one of the key distinctives of a pioneer: she totally believed in the innate qualities of her vision. In this case, each morning she would pour a trail of her strawberry essence along the pavement to lure the customers in.

Roddick was tempted to compromise on many occasions, but it was her core value, her *bigger* idea that she held on to, hence her statement:

> I'd rather promote human rights . . . than a bubble bath.[90]

Many tried to copy her success to which she responded, "If only they copied our principles and not just our products." [91]

Starting with a revelation, Roddick brought a new kind of ethical revolution to the malls and market places of the world. She resisted attempts to conform, and now The Body Shop has been reproduced all over the globe, either by herself or through the flattery of imitation. By 2004, The Body Shop had 1,980 stores worldwide, serving over 77 million customers. It was voted the 28th top brand in the world and, perhaps most importantly to its founder, the second most *trusted* brand in her nation.[92]

Even more explicitly demonstrating this paradigm is TOMS shoes.

Within the youth ministry that the Pais Project helped repurpose in Fort Worth, Texas, my team and I found that the most productive teachings were those which stretched the students. We challenged them that God was looking for people who would do things differently. We therefore took them through the four stages of *The Spirit of a Pioneer*, looking behind the scenes of Christianity and the politics they would face if they chose to swim upstream. In that particular teaching series, the current we challenged them to swim against was not that of secular culture, but of Christian line-dwelling culture.

In the first message of that series, I used the example of TOMS Shoes. At the time it was a very new for-profit company. TOMS sells a certain type of shoe, and for each pair purchased, they give another pair to a child in a developing country who has no shoes. On that first week, I asked them to raise their hands if they had heard of the brand. Less than five percent had. I showed them a documentary produced by the company in which the founder told the story of his enterprise and what he hoped to achieve. The video showed the TOMS team fitting masses of barefoot, poverty-stricken children with their first pair of shoes, bringing tears to the eyes of many students. After the video finished, I asked them what they thought his big vision was. Many of them said, "To give away free shoes to those who could not afford them."

I then explained to them that they were wrong. I pointed out something the CEO said that was bigger than just giving away shoes. He wanted to change the way the world's businesses think. He wanted to encourage other CEO's to adopt a policy of 'two for one.' He hoped to create an economic model where, for every unit of product purchased, a free unit could be given to someone in need.

It is a brilliant concept, and it could apply to absolutely anything: food, energy, medicine, housing, technology, transportation, communication. The possibilities are endless!

But nobody in that room had heard him say it, nobody got it, nobody realized it.

Yet, if this pioneer fulfilled his dream, giving away mere millions of free shoes would be a drop in the ocean. It would fade into insignificance when compared to what his idea could inspire others to do. Its significance would not be in its direct influence, but in its indirect influence.

It would be the extreme that influenced the mainstream.

Could your idea be bigger than you realize? If so, is it not worth pursuing?

Arrows

Psalm 127 helps me understand two dynamics I need to be aware of if my small idea is to affect the mainstream and grow bigger than I could ever imagine.

> *Unless the Lord builds the house, its builders labor in vain. Unless the Lord watches over the city, the watchmen stand guard in vain. In vain you rise early and stay up late, toiling for food to eat— for he grants sleep to those he loves.*[93]

Lynn and I have spent the last twenty-six years of marriage in a kind of role reversal. She is the practical one. If a shelf needs fixing, she will mend it, or if a wall needs painting, she's on it. Any handyman job and she's the woman of choice. When we walk around Home Depot, Lynn is the one inspecting the multi-drills, and I'm the one who points to a can of paint and makes comments like, "Oooh, salmon pink would be nice for the bathroom!"

I have no problem putting up a shelf. The shelf staying on the wall, however, that is the problem. So I totally understand *'builders laboring in vain'* to construct a house. After all, what is the point of working so hard if nothing lasts?

The second half of Psalm 127 provides the solution to the problem of that first half:

> *Sons are a heritage from the Lord, children a reward from him. Like arrows in the hands of a warrior are sons born in one's youth. Blessed is the man whose quiver is full of them. They will not be put to shame when they contend with their enemies in the gate.*[94]

Essentially, it is our successors who make our ideas stick. It is those who follow us, those we disciple or inspire, those in whom we reproduce our pioneering spirit that give longevity to what we have built. In Pais, it is the ones whose lives we touch that will then go on to touch the world.

Students are arrows we shoot into a future we cannot enter.

In my life, I can only fight with one opponent at a time in a hand-to-hand battle. But if I can reproduce what God has put in me, then I can destroy the work of the enemy in many other situations. I can shoot arrows into factories, offices, networks, societies, cultures, and governments that I can never physically walk into.

> *Houses can be robbed, cars can be wrecked, bodies can fall apart, stock markets can crash, but the reproduction of a God-given vision brings a joy that will never rust, be eaten away, broken into, or stolen.*[95]

Therefore, the joy of pioneering is most experienced in this final stage. It is this stage, however, that contains the final test . . .

Questions for the pioneer

1. What drops into your mind when you hear the word 'God'? Does this line up with how you see God? How might others be seeing this in you?

2. If it takes an extreme to influence the mainstream, can you live with being seen as an extremist? What does or does not bother you about this? How far must the mainstream shift to satisfy you?

3. Could your idea be bigger than you realize? In what ways do you imagine your dream being reproduced?

REPRODUCTION | Your Story

Matador

Reproduction #1: *Start with the end in mind!*

Count the cost to you. Count the cost to them. Count the cost to 'it.'

To finish what you start, you must start the way you want to finish.

A particular type of vine, known as the matador, grows in South America. Taking root at the base of a tree, the plant begins its vigorous climb to the top, wrapping itself around the trunk, digging into its bark, growing upwards higher and higher. But with its growth, the plant brings death as it sucks the life out of the tree on its ascent. Finally the matador reaches its goal, the top, and as it does so, it crowns itself with a flower.[96]

Any of us can succumb to the same temptation.

Yet truly successful pioneers do not simply create a path for their followers; they produce new pioneers. These new pioneers seek to take root under the shelter of our branches. Therefore, it is our responsibility to give our lives resourcing them, not sucking the resources from them in order to bring attention to ourselves. Sadly, however, some of the most successful people in the world are some of the most insecure people in the world.

Why?

Perhaps because they are afraid of losing the very thing they have worked so hard to achieve. However, we must be the ones who allow those with fresh revelation to grow up among us. We must be the first to believe in them and in their *'it.'* We must not be threatened by them or their ideas, and we must *affirm* them rather than *conform* them. With that in mind, here is a question to ask yourself no matter where you are on your journey:

What is your final aim?

To be the tree that bears fruit and seeds other trees, or to be the flower that sits upon the tree giving itself the glory? It all comes down to one word . . .

Control.

Mafia

Reproduction #2: *Don't do to others as others may have done to you.*

Do not patronize them. Do not persecute them. Do not purchase them.

At this stage of pioneering, we must never do to others what we believe was done to us.

Many years ago an incident made me think about the temptation I might face if Pais became recognized as a legitimate ministry. Back in Manchester, a group of youth and schools leaders had formed, and I was invited to become part of them. One day someone from the group suggested we create what could best be described as a Manchester Christian Schools Consortium. This sounded like a good idea . . . for a moment.

Then someone suggested we should 'vet' schools work in Manchester. The proposal was that since we were the ones working in schools, and since we had labored so hard to create the opportunities to do that, we should ensure that less experienced schools workers could not ruin it for the rest of us. We had earned the trust of the schools, so we should make sure that could never be jeopardized. In that meeting, an idea began to take shape. Novices would have to come and meet with us, convince us of their material, and allow us to ensure they met our standards. As the conversation went on, it dawned on me that I was about to become part of the hidden system that I had struggled against.

As the discussion gained momentum, I shared my concerns and ruled myself out. One or two others held up similar red flags, and eventually the proposal was killed off before it started.

Even then I realized that if you stay in the system too long, you may become part of it.

Mile

Reproduction #3: *Micro-manage the first mile.*

It is counter-intuitive. It seems counter-productive. It makes counter-demands.

So how do you grow a ministry, sticking to the ideals and beliefs that made you unique in the first place, but empowering and encouraging new pioneers to grow up through you?

Don't those two concepts compete with each other?

What I am about to suggest may seem odd, almost contradictory, but I promise it is not. At this stage, I need to take you back to the beginning. Do you remember my definition of a pioneer? A pioneer is someone who goes the extra mile . . . and then a little further. So, for a pioneer whom you are leading, the most significant thing they will ever do for the Kingdom is the one thing they do that you never told them to do. It is when they go off the page of what *you* have written for them. It is when they go beyond the path *you* set out for them.

Dangerous, eh?

Yet, it is the juxtaposition of this that allows them to do it.

You see, when people attempt to go the extra mile, they will do one of two things; they will either go the extra mile . . . or they will go the different mile.[97]

The different mile is when they ignore the first mile, therefore making their second mile a detour from the vision. For instance, let us say you are hosting a dinner party and you ask a member of your family to set up the plates, knives, and forks. You share with them your desire to create an evening of both culinary and aesthetic excellence.

If they go the *extra* mile, they will set up the plates, knives, and forks, and then, in line with your vision, they may find candles and candleholders to add to the atmosphere. You never asked them to, but they love and share your vision, so they go beyond what you asked them to do to fulfill more than what you expected of them.

If they go the *different* mile, however, they will ignore the request for the plates, knives, and forks and instead paint a beautiful picture to hang on the wall for your guests. As nice as that is, and even though it is going above and beyond what you asked, it is not what you or your guests needed. You asked them to provide the cutlery, but they love their vision, so they sidestep the first mile in order to fulfill the more attractive second mile they see.

What is the difference between people advancing the Kingdom or missing the point?

You are.

Now here's my peculiar advice:

> *You have to control the first mile if you want them to go the extra mile.*

You see, if you do not do what Jesus did and take people on the first mile, demonstrating and training them, then you will succumb to the eternal curse of corporate-style leadership. Corporate leadership does not put in the effort to train pioneers; it just uses people to fulfill its dreams. Under the guise of delegation, it gets people to do the jobs it does not want to do. Then because it has failed to invest itself in them, it spends much of its time correcting, controlling, and curbing the vision of those who inevitably go the different mile. Corporate leadership *releases* people into the first mile and then *controls* the second mile, whereas Kingdom leadership *controls* the first mile in order to fully *resource* people in the extra mile.

Reproducing pioneers is hard work.

When a newbie joins Pais, our best leaders are on them like a rash. True discipleship is pretty intense. I find that the more intention I put in now, the sooner I can set them free. I learned this from watching the life of my Master with His closest followers.

Jesus did the tough work of micro-managing the disciples for three years so that His Spirit could macro-manage them for two millennia.

Irony

Resistance #4: *Don't force what you think should happen; grasp onto what does!*

Don't be self-absorbed. Don't feel self-pity. Determine to do what works.

Sadly, people don't get behind my vision for the reasons I think they should.

According to the International Bible Society, 83% of all Christians made their commitment to Christ between the ages of four and fourteen, and evangelist Billy Graham is reported to have said that 90% of people who responded at his crusades are those who first came to the Lord as children or young people. You would think these facts alone would provide convincing proof for Christians to support, finance, and join us as we reach into schools.

After all, the Pais Project makes common sense. If you are eager to see God's Kingdom grow, then a ministry that touches people when they are still forming their worldview is surely a great thing to invest in! Not only that, but we freely use buildings that other people are financing, we are given huge kudos by serving alongside the established educational systems, and when we share our message, we are seen as a positive force for change by those we are reaching!

How often do you see that?

Surprisingly however, it is neither our work nor our effective strategy that attracts many people to get behind us. It is something unexpected.

It is our teaching.

Recently, we realized that those who have given us amazing resources and offered their skills and talents were first impacted by our books or came to love our alternative teaching on mission, discipleship, and study.

Ironically, the three distinctives, which hindered our appeal to many in the earlier stages of Pais, are now attracting far more people than they initially put off. It seems that the more we can get our teaching out, the more we are able to raise recruits and resources.

Once I discovered this, I changed my tactics. Rather than travel the world campaigning for our cause and arguing our case, I now work to create more books, training videos, and other tools.

I invest in what helps others grow, because being a tour guide to our teaching is much better than being a travel agent for their guilt trips.

The lesson?

Don't waste time moaning about what resources you believe your vision should entitle you to. Instead, run after the tell-tale signs of unexpected opportunities.

Barbs

Resistance #5: *Be prepared for it to all go right!*

Success may not feel like it. Success may not look like it. Success may be better than 'it.'

In the introduction to this book, we conjured up the image of a brave soldier throwing himself over a wall of barbed wire, in order that his band of brothers can walk over him and take the enemy's position. That's the way of a pioneer.

The barbs cut into us. They can cause us pain. They can disfigure us.

I have a good friend whom I have come to respect more and more over the years. Mark was born with an innate gift to make people laugh and communicate his thoughts. This led to his huge success as a public speaker. His calendar is constantly booked. He is courted by the largest conferences, churches, and platforms in his nation. He is, without doubt, a success.

Mark's ultimate desire is to connect people with a message of his faith. He is one of the most passionate people I know, and when a vision stays motivated by love, it inevitably becomes creative. Therefore, the more successful Mark has become in the eyes of his friends and colleagues, the more he has actually questioned the worth and effectiveness of what he does.

As a national evangelist, some of his awkward questions are:

> *Am I preaching to the choir? Have I become a tourist attraction for Christians? Is this the best way I can use my natural gifts?*

In his own estimation, although Mark was speaking to thousands, only the very fringe were his real audience, the ones he felt called and destined to connect with . . . those he refers to as "going to a forever without God." That's a heartbreaking conclusion to come to—the realization that although everyone else wishes they were you, you wish you were someone else. In Mark's case, he recognized it was not the healthy who needed a doctor, but the sick. He was called not to the righteous, but to the sinners of the world.[98]

So Mark had a revelation. Instead of simply making a living from touring churches and Christian conferences, speaking to large numbers of the choir but only handfuls of the fringe, he would find a different platform. He would create a comedy tour. Booking small venues that could hold just a few hundred, he created a one hour performance where he shared three adventures in his life, the third being a spiritual one. It was much riskier. It meant saying 'no' to the meat and potatoes of what he traditionally did and what paid his salary.

His vision began to take off, and importantly, the majority of those who were coming to hear him did not go to church and have probably never heard a message anything like the one Mark speaks.[99] But there are several barbs on which he will need to throw himself.

When I had the privilege of hearing my friend unpack a little bit more of his dream, he painted the picture of standing on stage in the major theaters of Britain and across the world. In my mind, he certainly has the gifting and talent to pull this off. Instead of reaching hundreds, he would speak to thousands upon thousands. Towards the end of our conversation, I felt prompted to ask him a question.

> What if you are the pioneer, and God uses you to create a new way, but then someone else comes along after all your hard work, and it is that person who tours the larger centers of the entertainment world?

It is a question I have to ask myself.

It is not a rule of the four stages that the pioneer will never be the one to become famous for creating the new way. It is, however, a strong possibility . . . a possibility that you need to come to peace with in order to pass the final test of pioneering.

When we first came to America, one person said to me, "Paul, you have to be careful about sharing the idea of Pais. The economic model is so compelling, the concept is so thrilling, and the implementation is so effective that someone else with much more resources may come along and steal the idea."

Yes . . . and the problem is?

Pioneer, before you walk the path, you may need to come to a place of peace with a possible scenario. A scenario where you may end your life as a bloody, trampled corpse, with barbs in your belly and footprints on your back, lying on a field that has long since been forgotten.

A pioneer does not just *make* a way. He *becomes* the way.

To be forewarned is to be forearmed.

Questions for the pioneer

4. Can you relate to the Matador Vine? How so?

5. Pioneering means to lie on barbed wire. Which barbs are you prepared to suffer?

6. What if you successfully pioneer your dream, but the recognition and accolades come to those who follow the path you forged? What is the response of your heart?

The Starfish and the Pioneer

Starfish

At the close of this first book in the Kingdom Trilogy, I would like to share with you a story that preachers love to tell, intending to motivate us to make a difference.

One day a man wanders onto a beach and notices a little boy trying to rescue thousands of starfish stranded on the sand. As he watches, time after time, the boy slowly and meticulously picks up a starfish and throws it back into the sea.

Seeing this, the man asks the boy, "Why are you bothering? There are thousands of starfish on the beach; you'll never be able to make a difference." But picking up yet another starfish, the little boy replies, "Yes, but I can make a difference to this one."

I hate the starfish story. I am with the adult—buy yourself a tractor!

Thousands of starfish are on the beach, and millions are dying without Christ. Now, of course, I understand the point is to encourage us that when we feel overwhelmed by the need, we can at least still impact the lives of some. But my problem is that I think the starfish story sends out an anti-pioneering message. It essentially says, *As long as I'm doing my bit, it's ok.*

Yet, sometimes our bit isn't good enough.

The challenge is not to build the biggest, most effective church in your city; the challenge is to reach your city. The call is not to feel you are doing your bit because you are doing better than anyone else; the call is to join others to do our collaborative best.

The truest questions force us to compare our actions not to one another, but to *Him*.

Line-dwelling just wants to make sure it satisfies the law. It is keen to fulfill the program, because the program has a clear start and finish. It is interested in the system rather than the spirit behind it.

However, the world does not need a new kind of *program*. It needs a new kind of *person*.

People who:

Seek a *revelation* although they may feel alone.

Cause a *revolution* although seen as a threat.

Join the *resistance* although pressured to surrender their idea.

Commit to *reproduction* although tempted with recognition.

And that takes a journey of faith, not a quick trip to glory.

According to a press release by Reuters some time back, Israel's National Park Authority approved plans for what would become the world's most bizarre tourist attraction. Jutting out from the beach in the Sea of Galilee, a submerged walkway entirely made of glass would provide tourists with a unique experience.

Can you guess what that experience would be?

It would be built to make them feel like they could walk on water. It was designed to be invisible. Transparent. The plan was that tourists could stroll along the attraction pretending to do what Jesus did. I'm not sure if that walkway was ever built, but if so, tourists could take photographs and video clips. YouTube, Facebook, and various other online sites would be able to catalogue their 'acts of faith.'

My point is simple . . .

Tourists don't walk on water. They only appear to.

Tourists cannot be pioneers. They aren't really walking by faith; something invisible is holding them up. They are determined to make a difference in the world, but they still want security, demanding that certain invisible supports are put into place for every step they take.

Finance. Status. Title. Credibility. Proof.

So they live on a line, often confined by the very restrictions they have put in place to protect themselves. They only go where it is safe to go. They only tread where others have trod. They only believe what others tell them will work.

But is God's purpose for the four stages of pioneering to carefully dismantle the glass walkways beneath us?

I think it may be.

I believe God is determined to take you on a journey where the four stages of pioneering do not trip up your faith, but instead spur it on. So for those of you who have given up hope that the Kingdom can be advanced in your life, your community, or your world, take note of the fact that all things are possible when you go beyond yourself . . . when you go further than what is written for you by others.

You will walk off the glass walkway and so far beyond the line, that when you look back, you will see . . .

The line has become a mere dot.

NOTES

A Note from the Publisher

When people read the first edition of this book, many said they wanted to read it again to better grasp the plethora of ideas it contained. So, this second edition is designed to be re-read in a different order. If you would like to go through it again also, then try this: read all the My Story chapters, then all the Our Story chapters, and then all the Your Story chapters. It will still make sense and give you a slightly different perspective.

Tell us what you think! Share your thoughts in an Amazon review and like our page on Facebook.com/harrishousepublishing.

Endnotes

1. Matthew 5:41.

2. J. Hudson Taylor, *Hudson Taylor (Men of Faith)* (Ada, MI: Bethany House, 1987).

3. Jackie Pullinger, *Chasing the Dragon: One Woman's Struggle against the Darkness of Hong Kong's Drug Dens* (Ventura, CA: Regal Book, 2007).

4. Loren Cunningham with Janice Rogers, *Is That Really You, God?* (Seattle: YWAM Publishing, 2001).

5. Martin Luther King, Jr., Washington, DC, August 28th, 1963, during the march on Washington.

6. Winston Churchill, during the Battle of Britain, August 20th, 1940.

7. Jesus Christ, John 14:6.

8. Hebrews 12:1-3 (*The Message*).

9. Matthew 11:12 (NLT).

10. For some interesting insight into this, see *The Sage from Galilee*. David Flusser with R. Steven Notely, *The Sage from Galilee* (Grand Rapids: Wm. D. Earmans Publishing Company, 2007), 31.

11. Merriam-Webster entry for 'pioneer' found at www.merriam-webster.com.

12. You can read more about this and the surprising twists in our engagement in another book of the Kingdom Trilogy, *Kingdom Principles*.

13. One of these, Paul Morley, was particularly helpful in equipping me and generously passing on all that he had learned in his outreach to schools.

14. The men were Mormons.

15. Strong's Bible Concordance reference #3816. James Strong, *Strong's Exhaustive Concordance of the Bible* (Nashville: Thomas Nelson, 2010).

16. Luke 18:38; Mark 10:47.

17. John 1:10.

18. Mark 10:51.

19. My loose paraphrase of the awkward conversation between God and Moses in Exodus 3:10-4:17.

20. Acts 9:4-5.

21. The building was for a youth ministry called Oneighty, the 7th-12th grade ministry of Church On The Move located in Tulsa, Oklahoma.

22. Proverbs 29:18.

23. Luke 2:49-50.

24. Yes, we got married, and now I call her The Foxy Lynn.

25. You may notice that the Gospel accounts appear to contradict themselves. Some say Jesus was entering Jericho, others that He was leaving it. That is because there were two Jerichos, the old and new cities. The road that linked them was heavy with traffic and therefore the optimum place for beggars to gather. Bartimaeus was one of many beggars that day.

26. For further insight, see http://en.wikipedia.org/wiki/Healing_the_blind_near_Jericho.

27. Stormrider Guides consist of a full series devoted to finding the world's most surfable coastlines.

28. Damon Hill first became a Formula One racing driver with Williams F1 Team in 1992. He won the championship in 1996, and retired in 1999. For more information, check out his entry on Wikipedia.

29. Luke 5:4-7.

30. Lisa eventually married her highschool sweetheart Pete. They now have two children and continue to serve God in the Midlands.

31. The estimated number of youth leaving the Church in the UK between 1990 and 2020 is 1.1 million according to Christian Research UK.

32. *Kingdom Principles*, another book in the Kingdom Trilogy, fully unpacks the Kingdom Principles series. It helps people see that line-dwelling (the do's and don'ts of rule following) vanishes when we ask, "What exactly is in the heart of the King?"

33. In the UK, schools were required to teach the six world faiths: Christianity, Judaism, Hinduism, Sikhism, Islam, and Buddhism.

34. Mishnah Tractate Avot 1:1.

35. Matthew 12:9-14.

36. Genesis 1:1.

37. 1 John 4:8.

38. Survey taken by the International Bible Society.

39. Mark 9:38-40.

40. I once heard Paul Scanlon of Life Church in Bradford, UK, say this.

41. Thomas Jefferson, "Jefferson's Letter to the Danbury Baptists" (January 1, 1802). U.S. Library of Congress.

42. You guessed it...I'm an Apple guy!

43. Matthew 12:1-2.

44. Ephesians 6:12.

45. Matthew 5:39.

46. For a greater understanding of Jesus' illustration and its basis in competition, not conflict, see *Meet the Rabbis*. Brad H. Young, *Meet the Rabbis: Rabbinic Thought and Teachings of Jesus* (Ada: Baker Academic, 2007), 209-210.

47. For examples of how God rewards those who Seek First the Kingdom of God, please check out *Kingdom Principles*, another book in this Kingdom Trilogy.

48. Coca-Cola CEO Donald R. Keough, "Passion: Life's Single Most Important Ingredient," Commencement address, Emory University, May 10, 1993.

49. Matthew 10:26.

50. Isaiah 54:2.

51. Approximately $279,000.

52. Approximately $75,000.

53. Rick Warren, partially quoting former US president Harry S. Truman. Rick Warren, *The Purpose Driven Church: Growth Without Compromising Your Message & Mission,* (Grand Rapids: Zondervan, 1995).

54. 1 Samuel 17:39.

55. 1 Samuel 17:36.

56. Rebecca Grace, "'Church? No Thanks.' Why Teens are leaving in droves," *AFA Journal,* May 2008.

57. Talmud, Kesuvos 5a.

58. Before they fully understood He was God, they may have initially believed He was a good rabbi to follow; some may have understood He was the Messiah.

59. You can find out more about our Bible study distinctive by reading my book *Haverim: The Four Lost Levels of Study* (Harris House Publishing, 2013).

60. John 6:14-15.

61. Matthew 4:8-9.

62. People often complain about the Bible, pointing to its many seeming contradictions. For instance in the temptation of Jesus recorded in Luke 4:1-13, the order of Jesus' temptations are different from Matthew's account. To merge both gospel accounts into one is to lose the point of the contradictions. Each gospel writer was bringing out a different facet of all the things Jesus accomplished. Why did Jesus do what we should not? Because only Jesus was able to overcome Satan in this way. In fact...it was His purpose! Look for contradictions; they can be significant. Sometimes God encourages us to do one thing yet seems to allow something else to happen to us. Contradiction is confusing, but it can lead to clarity if we seek Him hard enough rather than walk away. (See *Hard Sayings of the Bible* by Walter C. Kaiser, Jr., et al.)

63. Encarta Online Encyclopedia entry for 'compromise.'

64. This was a quote in one of the major national tabloids in England. To emphasize their point, the reporters from this particular newspaper also pointed out that some of the teenagers had never seen a cow.

65. Approximately $3,250.

66. Approximately $19,500.

67. Approximately $26,000.

68. Approximately $101,000.

69. Matthew 6:31.

70. Based on the example of Paul the Apostle, 'tent-making' is a phrase used for a job [usually secular] that is undertaken to financially support that person's unequivocal spiritual ministry.

71. Traditionally, a tithe (from Old English: teogoþa meaning "tenth") is one-tenth of one's earnings, paid as a contribution to a religious organization.

72. There is a reason for this that I will discuss in the third book of this trilogy about Kingdom Patterns.

73. Genesis 1:28.

74. For more background and interesting insights into the origins of some of our modern day practices, take a look at *Pagan Christianity* by Frank Viola and George Barna.

75. Matthew 28:19.

76. Pais was founded in 1992.

77. We created 'Livewire,' a weekly one hour teaching video with interactive workshops that every Pais team around the world would watch and train symbiotically. We used social media not only to connect with each other, but to shine a light on any particular success a nation saw, and adopt that latest idea. Livewire is now an open source resource, and you can view all series for free by visiting www.mypais.com.

78. Joel 2:28.

79. *The Spirit of a Pioneer* by Windward Productions is a feature length documentary film about the four stages of vision. Inspired by this book, *Kingdom Pioneering*, the film documents the progress of Kingdom pioneers on Pais, and it is available to watch for free at www.thespiritofapioneer.com.

80. The real name of Mr. S. is withheld for safety reasons.

81. 'Haverim' is defined as 'friends who study together.' Kevin implemented haverim groups in his church, using Pais' key Bible study distinctive, Haverim Devotions, which is fully described in my book, *Haverim: The Four Lost Levels of Study* (Harris House Publishing, 2013).

82. Learn more about the Pais degree program at www.paisproject.com/optional-upgrades.

83. Based on 1 John 4:19, which declares, "We love because he first loved us," the *Because You're Loved* initiative inspires people to perform anonymous good deeds for others. Find out how you can get involved at www.becauseyoureloved.com and look for the *Because You're Loved* book by Mark Nathan Riley on amazon.

84. A. W. Tozer.

85. Acts 2:43-47.

86. These two words are taken from *The Five Stages of Pais*, a document outlining the five stages of impact a Pais national team can have on their nation, as well as the five stages that an idea goes through. I teach this as part of a series on Pioneering.

87. Swampy's real name was the very conservative sounding Daniel Hooper.

88. John 14:12.

89. Jacqueline L. Salmon, "Pew Maps Muslim Populations Worldwide," *The Washington Post Online*. October 8, 2008.

90. Taken from a speech by Roddick at the Academy of Management, Vancouver, August 1995.

91. Anita Roddick, *Sunday Telegraph*, February 3, 1995.

92. 1999 vote by the Consumers Association. Interestingly, on March 17, 2006, Roddick sold The Body Shop for £652 million, causing all manner of controversies since L'Oreal (the buyer) tests its products on animals. Had Roddick injected a Trojan horse as she hoped into one of the conglomerates of the world, or had she succumbed bizarrely to the third test of a pioneer? Only time will tell. What we do know is that she died eighteen months later on September 10, 2007.

93. Psalm 127:1-2.

94. Psalm 127:3-5.

95. This is my paraphrase of Matthew 6:19-21.

96. 'Matador Vine' is one of the common names of the Bladderflower (*Araujia sericifera*) – also referred to as the 'cruel plant.'

97. The phrase, "a different mile," was first used by Chris Cunnington, one of the Pais directors, as I taught on this at a Global Summit.

98. Mark 2:17 (paraphrased).

99. Mark is currently touring with his own one man evangelistic theatre show, mixing his unique blend of humor with the Gospel message. For more information visit www.73rdtrust.com.

About the Pais Movement

Our Aim

Pais exists to spark a global movement, where the primary concern of God's people is His Kingdom, and where they are equipped to advance it in their world. We do this through distinctive approaches to mission, discipleship, and study in the areas of youth & schools, churches, and business.

Our Passion

Pais is the New Testament Greek word for 'child' or 'child servant to the king.' Our motto is "missionaries making missionaries." We are passionate about the people of our world and are desperate to see them in the relationship with God that He intended us to have. We come alongside schools, churches, and businesses in their endeavor to empower people to grow in their understanding and experience of God.

Our Vision

Mission lies at the heart of Pais. We seek to help both the apprentices and those they touch develop missionary hearts, missionary skills, and missionary lives. As each missionary makes a missionary, we see our world change.

www.paismovement.com
www.facebook.com/paismovement
www.twitter.com/paismovement

About the Author

Paul Gibbs is the founder and global director of Pais. He and his wife Lynn have two sons, Joel and Levi. Originally from Manchester, England, the Gibbs family moved to the USA in 2005 to globally expand Paul's vision of "missionaries making missionaries."

Paul began pioneering openings into Manchester schools as an associate minister in 1987. In September 1992, he founded the Pais Project, initially a one team gap year project in north Manchester, which has exploded globally, training and placing thousands of missionaries and reaching millions of students throughout Europe, North and South America, Asia, Africa, and Australia. Since then, Paul has developed two other branches of Pais: one that equips churches in missional strategies and one that provides businesses with cause marketing strategies. Under Paul's leadership, the Pais Movement continues to grow, launching initiatives and resources to further God's Kingdom.

Paul gained national recognition in the UK for mentoring and training leaders. He has written three books and speaks throughout the world on topics which include pioneering, leadership development, the Kingdom of God, and ancient practices for post-modern times.

Paul enjoys swimming, surfing, skiing, sailing, and snowboarding, and he is an avid Manchester United fan!

www.paulgibbs.info
www.facebook.com/paulcgibbs
www.twitter.com/paulcgibbs

See the documentary film inspired by this book . . .

'THE SPIRIT
of a
PIONEER'

a film about the four stages of vision

'Inspirational & Informative!'
Based on the book "The Line and the Dot" by Paul Clayton Gibbs

TheSpiritofaPioneerFilm.com
Free to view on **vimeo**

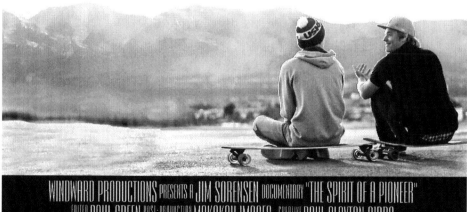

Other Books by Paul Clayton Gibbs

The Ancient Trilogy

Haverim: How to Study Anything with Anyone
This unique book teaches you how to explore Scripture with those of no faith, little faith, or even another faith. Providing step-by-step guidance, Paul Gibbs equips you to launch your own Bible study using Haverim Devotions.™

Talmidim: How to Disciple Anyone in Anything
Helping us fundamentally rethink our current methods of discipleship, Paul Gibbs gives a fresh understanding of the Great Commission. By researching and applying Jesus's method of discipleship, Gibbs provides a simple template anyone can use.

Shalom: How to Reach Anyone Anywhere
Offering a fresh approach to missions, this book will help you learn how to spread the gospel naturally and effectively.

The Kingdom Trilogy

Kingdom Pioneering: Fulfill God's Calling
Presenting four stages that everyone must pass through to accomplish their God-given dreams, Paul Gibbs helps you navigate the challenges of each phase in order to fulfill God's calling.

Kingdom Principles: Develop Godly Character
Unpacking six Kingdom Principles that will transform your relationships with God and others, Paul Gibbs teaches you how to think, not what to think, in order to develop a Godly character.

Kingdom Patterns: Discover God's Direction
Offering five diagrams that show the ways in which God guides us, Paul Gibbs teaches you how to find the next step in your pursuit of God's will.

Available through harrishousepublishing.com and amazon.com.

/paulcgibbs

Printed in Great Britain
by Amazon

41202611R00088